Complete Guide to

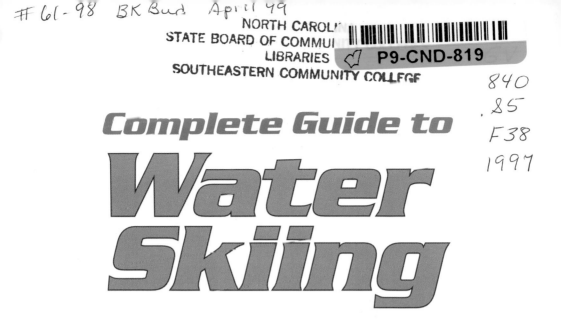

Water Skiing

Ben Favret
Bennett's Water Ski School

David Benzel
Winning Ways Enterprises

Human Kinetics

Library of Congress Cataloging-in-Publication Data

Favret, Ben, 1965-
    Complete guide to water skiing / Ben Favret, David Benzel.
        p.   cm.
    ISBN 0-88011-522-X
    1. Water skiing.   I. Benzel, David, 1949-   . II. Title.
    GV840.S5F38   1997
    797.3'5--dc21   96-40091
                                                                     CIP

ISBN: 0-88011-522-X

Cover photo and all interior photos provided by Doug DuKane.

Developmental Editor: Marni Basic; **Assistant Editors:** Alesha G. Thompson and John Wentworth; **Editorial Assistants:** Amy Carnes and Jennifer Hemphill; **Copyeditor:** Bob Replinger; **Proofreader:** Erin T. Cler; **Graphic Designer:** Judy Henderson; **Graphic Artists:** Angela K. Snyder and Judy Henderson; **Photo Editor:** Boyd LaFoon; **Cover Designer:** Jack Davis; **Illustrator:** Sara Wolfsmith; **Printer:** United Graphics

Human Kinetics books are available at special discounts for bulk purchase. Special editions or book excerpts can also be created to specification. For details, contact the Special Sales Manager at Human Kinetics.

Printed in the United States of America   10   9   8   7   6   5   4   3   2   1

Human Kinetics
Web site: http://www.humankinetics.com/

United States: Human Kinetics, P.O. Box 5076, Champaign, IL 61825-5076
1-800-747-4457
e-mail: humank@hkusa.com

Canada: Human Kinetics, Box 24040, Windsor, ON N8Y 4Y9
1-800-465-7301 (in Canada only)
e-mail: humank@hkcanada.com

Europe: Human Kinetics, P.O. Box IW14, Leeds LS16 6TR, United Kingdom
(44) 1132 781708
e-mail: humank@hkeurope.com

Australia: Human Kinetics, 57A Price Avenue, Lower Mitcham, South Australia 5062
(08) 277 1555
e-mail: humank@hkaustralia.com

New Zealand: Human Kinetics, P.O. Box 105-231, Auckland 1
(09) 523 3462
e-mail: humank@hknewz.com

To Yvette and my mother.
Thank you for your love, devotion and faith.

Ben Favret

To every skier who dreams of harder tricks,
longer jumps, or shorter rope; for it shall be done.

David Benzel

Photos in *Complete Guide to Water Skiing* were made possible in part by Correct Craft, manufacturers of Ski Nautique, the World's #1 Choice.

CONTENTS

CHAPTER 1

DEVELOPING YOUR WATER SKIING SKILLS

SKIING SAFETY AND EQUIPMENT

WATER SKIING FITNESS

BASIC SKIING SKILLS

CHAPTER 5
SLALOM SKIING

CHAPTER 6

TRICK SKIING, WAKEBOARDING, AND KNEEBOARDING

CHAPTER 7

JUMP SKIING

COMPETITION

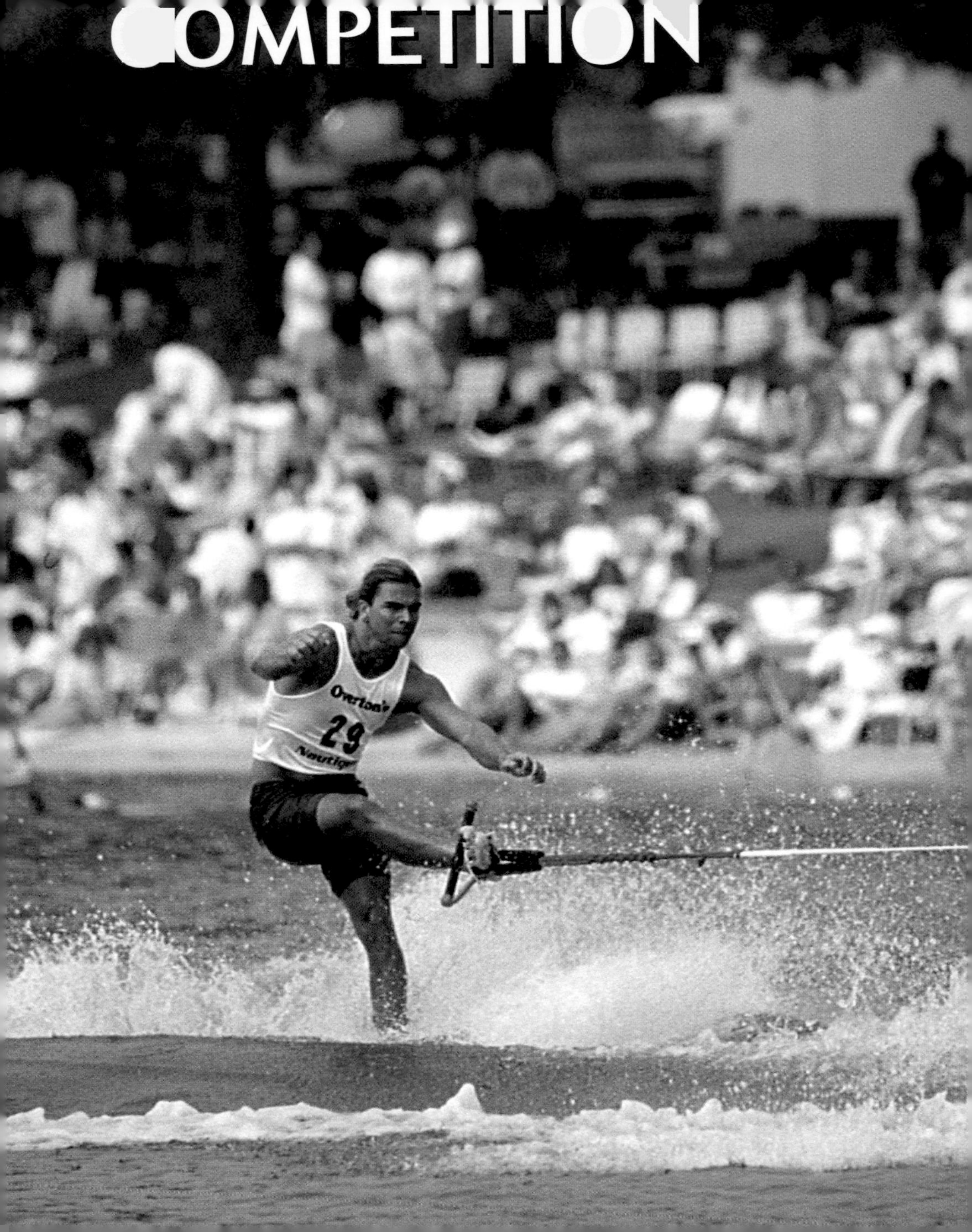

CHAPTER 9

MENTAL TOUGHNESS AND TRAINING STRATEGIES

FINE-TUNING YOUR SKIING SKILLS

PREFACE

Some people say water skiing is the most free and exciting activity they've ever done—the biggest thrill they've ever had. We agree—the pure enjoyment of skiing is why we got into it in the first place. Skiing can also be challenging, if that's what you're looking for. In fact, it seems that no matter how skilled you get at water skiing, there's always somebody out there who's doing something you've never tried before.

If you've skied a while and it's a challenge you want, this book can help you build your skills and take your skiing to the next level. If you're new to water skiing, we'll tell you what you need to know about equipment and present information on such things as boat driving and safety, beginning tricks, and learning how to run the slalom course.

That you have picked up and brought home this book shows that you're ready to learn more about an activity that can be enjoyed by nearly everyone. Our goal in this book is to help you become the water skier *you want to be*. Maybe you're a weekend skier who hops in the car with your family and heads to Lake Winnipusuket every other Saturday to teach your kids to ski. Maybe you have been skiing a few years just for fun, and circumstances now allow you to spend more time on the water—you're ready to learn new skills and possibly even enter competitions. Or maybe you're already a competitive skier with thousands of hours on the water, and you're looking for training tips and fresh ideas to help you maintain your enthusiasm. Whatever your goals as a water skier, this book will help you achieve them. Because the book is about building skills—creating a foundation and adding to it by learning new things and fine-tuning your abilities—the material is appropriate for anyone who skis, novices and experts alike.

The book's 10 chapters move you from developing basic water skiing skills and learning about equipment, fitness, and safety to specifics about slalom, tricks, and jump. The last chapters are devoted to helping you acquire mental toughness and polishing your skills. Along the way, you'll pick up necessary instruction and useful tips that will help you gain confidence and increase your skills at an appropriate pace. This book can be either your starting place for a new and exciting activity or a handbook to consult as you hone your skills. So, read on—take a step toward becoming the water skier you want to be!

ACKNOWLEDGMENTS

None of my dreams could have or will come true without the help, support, love, and dedication of my family and friends. I thank you all for being on "My Dream Team": Jay & Anne Bennett (and you, too, Danielle!); the entire Bennett's Pro Team & Staff, but especially Chris, Freddy, JD, Mike, Donny, TO, Joe, Jeff, Scot, Sherri, and Lynda; Steve Schnitzer; Andy Mapple; Chris Blase; Dan Wilbanks; Stewart Springer; Fred Kam; Kenny Lacour; Kirk Schmidt; Steve Driscoll; Dave Benzel; Martin Barnard; Marni Basic; Ted Miller; Doug "Da Dog" DuKane; Bob Reich; Larry Meddock; Andre Favret; Eric Neuman; Todd Witherall; Ty; Fish; Kook; Jocko; King; Fawn; and, last but not least, Captain Bligh.

You have all given me the the most special gift anyone can receive by making my dreams come true. Thank you!

—Ben Favret

A success model is someone, or some organization, that exudes the attributes we all admire. I have been personally and professionally blessed through my relationship with three such organizations and their people who make things happen. The extra efforts and dependability of Correct Craft, O'Brien, and World Publications (*Water Ski* magazine) made a project like this feasible. I am proud to know them. My thanks to Ben Favret for his commitment to every detail and for accepting the challenge.

—Dave Benzel

CHAPTER 1

DEVELOPING YOUR WATER SKIING SKILLS

"Whether you think you can or you think you can't, you're probably right."

Henry Ford

The Tchefuncte River winds like an 11-mile long snake through the pine forest and cypress swamps of St. Tammany Parish before it reaches Lake Ponchatrain on the Northshore of New Orleans. The hours I spent on the silty waters of the Tchefuncte are some of the finest memories I have. I vividly recall two events on the Tchefuncte River that, unbeknownst to me at the time, shaped my life. The first came at age four. My father, the self-proclaimed king of the river (he once did a hundred 360s on a disc), decided it was time for his first child to learn to ski. Believe me, it didn't take much persuasion to get my hyperactive skinny little butt to try it. My dad held me in position just off the beach area we called the pavilion, and the driver blasted the 40-horsepower Johnson mounted on a 13-foot flatboat into gear.

My skiing career did not begin gloriously. I popped out of the water, cruised about 50 yards to the middle of the river, and planted my face right between the skis. This eye-peeling fall taught me the importance of two things in skiing—a good instructor and a good driver. I decided, as I floated in the river trying to focus my eyes and clear my head, that

1

I would wait until I had more confidence in my crew before attempting to water ski again, but damn, this is fun.

My second life-altering event occurred during the summer after eighth grade. I had finally found the driver and instructor who could get me hydroplaning proficiently, and I spent the summer playing on the river and "working" on the new house we were building. Until this point we lived in New Orleans, and reaching the river required a weekend excursion. Now we were moving to the river, and I could not wait to tear up the water every day. This is when I became addicted to water skiing. I read every page of *Spray,* the big ski magazine at the time. I knew who all the top skiers were. I dreamed of skiing a slalom course or launching off a ramp. What a great summer—acting like Bob LaPoint cranking out slalom turns and throwing up a huge wall of water that soaked the entire dock . . . cutting at the wakes and giving them a kick that propelled me through the air as if I were Wayne Grimnich. I was the king of the river now, and if you didn't believe me, all you had to do was ask me.

That is precisely what this book is about, learning how to make your water skiing dreams come true—how to take your water skiing performance to that ever elusive next level, how to do that new flip, how to run your dream pass in slalom, or how to bust that big jump out into space where you have never been before. This book is about taking your skills—physically, mentally, and technically—to a new level so you can accomplish your goals and be the skier you dream of being. Carl Roberge, Andy Mapple, Kristi Overton, Sherri Slone—they were not born with supernatural talent to make the impossible possible on the water. They trained and worked on the skills needed to accomplish these transcendental feats of athletic prowess. You, too, can develop the skills needed to turn your skiing up a notch.

By following the training program presented in this book you can achieve your desired level of performance and make your dreams a reality.

GETTING INTO THE LEARNING MINDSET

In this first chapter we will lay the foundation for future learning and give a brief overview of the information covered in the book. First, we must prepare our minds for learning. In their book *Thinking Body, Dancing Mind,* Jerry Lynch and Chunglaing Al Huang speak of the "beginner's mind." The idea is simple: "Open yourself up to your unlimited potential for achievement, rid yourself of all the overused and undernourishing ideas you have inherited about athletics, business, and life. By opening your mind and being receptive you invite many new attitudes on which you can build a solid foundation for learning and become aware of a multitude of alternate avenues that lead to extraordinary performance." Simply stated, you must realize how much you do not know to be able to learn more. An anecdote makes the point and reveals the essence of the beginner's mind.

A successful skier went to the water ski guru and announced he had come to learn all about skiing. The guru invited the skier to sit and have tea. As the guru poured the tea, it overflowed. The skier shouted, "It's spilling, it's spilling!" To which the guru replied, "Precisely. You came with a full cup. Your cup is already spilling over, so how can I give you anything? Unless you come with emptiness, I can give you nothing."

CHARTING YOUR COURSE

Now that your cup is empty, set your mind for learning. You are now ready to be filled with knowledge that will give you the confidence, courage, and motivation to achieve your goals. Let's get to work on charting your course for success. In his book *The Inner Athlete*, Dan Millman suggests that we can choose from three paths of skill development, illustrated in figure 1.1.

Curve A is the erratic, inconsistent pattern of most skiers. These skiers improve rapidly at first, but as skill requirements advance, fundamental weaknesses begin to have an increasing influence on performance. These skiers plateau because insufficient preparation has built a weak talent foundation. Often these skiers feel they have reached their

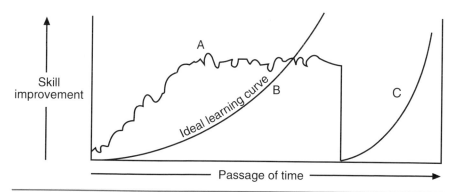

Figure 1.1   Three skill development learning curves.
Reprinted, by permission, from Chapter 3 "Preparation," *Inner Athlete*, Dan Millman, Stillpoint Publishing, Walpole, N.H. 03608.

potential or are too old for the sport, and motivation wanes as frustration increases because of lack of improvement.

Curve B is the path of the total skier. At first progress is slow, and the training is initially difficult with little progress. These skiers are working "below the waterline," developing a hidden foundation. Gradually but surely the learning curve begins to turn upward, until progress accelerates at a rapid, consistent, and almost effortless pace. By spending time doing the grunt work on fundamentals, these skiers also establish confidence, courage, persistence, and the ability to adapt to any situation they may face in competition. If you coach a child, use this approach but keep the focus on having fun rather than performing under pressure.

Curve C is the most important because it represents the second chance we always wanted. If you have been riding the roller coaster of curve A and have reached a plateau, or if you feel your preparation has been insufficient, you can duplicate the path of the natural skier by going back for a time—maybe a few months—to do intense work on your talent foundation. In his book *I Can't Accept Not Trying*, Michael Jordan observes that "you have to monitor your fundamentals constantly because the only thing that changes is your attention to them. The fundamentals never change." The same idea applies to water skiing. It takes the patience of Job to start over, but failing to take the time to develop proper fundamentals is often what keeps you from accomplishing your goals.

BUILDING YOUR TALENT FOUNDATION

What is a talent foundation and how do you build one? Your talent foundation encompasses three components: (1) physical fitness, (2) technical skills and drills development, and (3) mental toughness skills. These pillars of performance are held together by a fourth factor, sport nutrition. Whether you are concerned with fitness, skills, competition, or nutrition, a progressive, step-by-step approach to the task at hand can ensure success. Each of these pillars of performance can be broken down into a series of small steps that together represent a gradual, methodical process leading you to success. This is precisely how we present information in this book. We have added special sections on equipment, coaching, driving, training techniques, and treating and preventing injuries to give you the knowledge to train with more enjoyment and fewer frustrations.

A RECIPE FOR SUCCESS

U.S. Water Ski Team coach Jay Bennett uses the analogy of baking a cake when talking about what it takes to get to the next level of water ski performance. This is Jay's recipe for the ideal skier.

Start by preheating the oven with desire. Next, get your ingredients together:

4 cups of self-discipline
2 cups of physical ability
1 cup of focus
1 ounce of knowledge

This award-winning recipe begins with a body full of desire. No recipe will work without a preheated oven! You must wake up every morning with the desire to be better than you were the day before and to train harder. Always be excited and ready to give 100 percent.

Next, you mix your ingredients. Start with self-discipline, the flour. You must be willing to make sacrifices and be dedicated to achieving your goals. Add some physical ability, the eggs, along with the ability to focus, the milk. This is what keeps cake together. Any coach can tell you that the ability to concentrate is present in every great athlete. Next, add the knowledge of how to train properly, the chocolate. It is common for a professional athlete to have the assistance of several coaches and trainers. You must get the right balance of physical, technical, mental, and nutritional training to be successful, just as only you know what type of chocolate you like.

Now for the icing—no cake is complete without it! It has just three ingredients: opportunity, support, and fun. Mix these ingredients and pour over the cake as taste dictates.

All skiers must have the opportunity to ski, the proper facilities, and support from family, friends, and coaches. We all have bad days, and that extra push or hug makes those hard times a little easier to deal with. I don't know anyone who has made it to the top alone. You need love and support from those close to you. When your support group sacrifices and makes a major effort , you must realize this and work with them. The last ingredient is the fun, the sugar. This is what makes it all worthwhile. To create a prize-winning cake, you must have fun. You must enjoy the daily successes and failures and learn from them as you achieve your goals.

No matter how much you know or how good you are, you can always improve. Many athletes we see on television have reached a high level of physical fitness or skill, but many have not yet realized their full potential because they have not benefited from being aware of their shortcomings. Consequently, they have never gone back to build their talent foundation. The beginner's mind can help you become like an empty cup ready to be filled with the confidence, courage, and motivation offered in this program. Now it is your turn to take control and decide how you will respond to Henry Ford's statement "Whether you think you can or you think you can't, you're probably right." Say "Yes, I can! Yes, I will!" And take your first step toward success.

Figure 1.2   Fun is an essential ingredient that makes your work worthwhile.

CHAPTER 2

SKIING SAFETY AND EQUIPMENT

In water skiing, as in all sports, safety is a function of taking time to prevent problems and preparing for them if they do arise. If you were a football player, you wouldn't go onto a football field without your helmet, and as a skier, you shouldn't take off from the dock without your life jacket. You may not think that safety is an interesting topic, but as long as people continue to violate the commonsense rules of water skiing safety and end up injured, no one can ignore it. In the following pages we'll review the rules of water skiing safety. Make sure that both you and the members of your boat crew know them.

WATER SKIING SAFETY RULES

Even if you have read these rules before and feel you are competent, please take a few minutes to go through them again. Maybe you will pick up something new or refresh yourself on something you forgot. Either way, it is worth taking a few minutes now rather than ruining a great day at the lake.

RULE 1: Always wear a flotation device that fits properly and will not slip off. A type III U.S. Coast Guard-approved personal flotation device (PFD) is recommended.

RULE 2: Check your equipment to ensure that it is in proper working condition. Inspect your skis for sharp or jagged edges, or loose binding or fin screws. Replace or repair torn life jackets, frayed ropes, or any other damaged equipment before someone gets hurt.

RULE 3: Give the signal to start only after the driver has removed the slack line from the rope and you are sure you are clear of any docks, logs, or other obstructions.

RULE 4: *Do not* ski near docks, pilings, other boats, or swimmers. Always keep your eyes looking ahead of you so you see what is coming. Don't be one of those fools who incur an avoidable water ski injury—a collision with a dock or solid object.

RULE 5: Never put any part of your body through the handle or wrap the line around you in any way without a trick release and a competent pin person.

RULE 6: Never ski in shallow water or in an area where there may be obstructions above or just beneath the surface.

RULE 7: When a fall is inevitable, try to fall backward or to either side.

RULE 8: Know and use the skier hand signals demonstrated in figure 2.1.

RULE 9: If you fall in an area where there is boat traffic, lift one ski more than halfway out of the water as a signal to other boaters.

RULE 10: Stop skiing before excessive fatigue sets in.

RULE 11: Ski only during daylight, from sunrise to one-half hour before sunset. It's the law.

RULE 12: Never ski in front of another boat.

RULE 13: Always use equal-length ropes when skiing doubles.

RULE 14: Always turn the boat's motor off when a skier is entering the boat from the water.

RULE 15: Always have an observer in the towboat.

RULE 16: Be aware of local ordinances and laws.

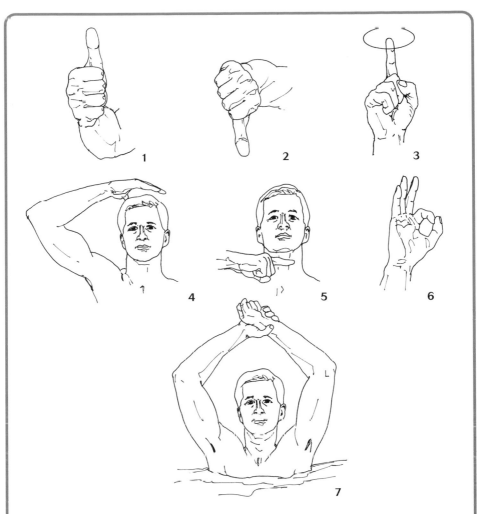

1. **Speed up**—The thumbs-up signal means the skier would like to increase the boat speed.
2. **Slow down**—The thumbs-down signal means the skier would like to decrease the boat speed.
3. **Turn**—When the skier or the driver wants to turn the boat around, he or she uses a circular motion with the hand over the head and one finger in the air. Whoever gave the signal then usually points in the direction of the turn.
4. **Back to dock**—A pat on the head indicates that the skier would like to return to the dock.
5. **Cut motor/stop**—A slashing motion across the neck means the boat is to stop immediately. This signal is used by the skier, observer, and driver.
6. **OK**—When the boat speed and path are good, the skier uses the OK signal by making an O with the index finger and thumb. The skier or observer also uses this signal to let the other know that signals have been received.
7. **"I'm OK" after a fall**—Clasp both hands over the head to let the boat crew know that you are not injured. It is important to give this signal after every fall.

Figure 2.1   Skier hand signals. Courtesy of the American Water Ski Association.

BOAT CREW

On the Pro Tour one of the most critical jobs is boat driver, and the same can be said for any weekend outing to the lake. As the captain of the ship, the boat driver is responsible for the safety of the skier and the crew. The driver's performance, attitude, and safety will set the example for the crew to follow. In the following sections, we'll provide driving tips and review driving and observing basics.

Driving Tips

As with any learned skill, the only way to become a great boat driver is to spend time behind the wheel and keep your ears and mind open to recommendations to improve your driving. Here are seven tips to improve your driving, no matter what your ability.

1. Think of the skier. Each skier deserves the best pull you can give regardless of their ability. Pay attention to the skier's size, weight, and skiing style. Learn to develop a feel of where the skier pulls and adapt your driving to it.

2. Know the local conditions. Take time before you pull the skier to figure out the boat path and pattern that minimizes backwash and boat rollers, while giving the skier the longest, straightest setups possible. Once you determine the best pattern, follow it exactly each time. By doing so you will create smooth water, develop familiarity and consistency, and have less chance of hitting anything in the water.

3. Test the boat before you pull the first skier. Check for handling characteristics, acceleration, and overall responsiveness. If the boat is not adequate or if you cannot fix the problems, get another boat or find a driver who can adapt to the boat's style. Under no circumstances should you let your ego get in the way of taking yourself out of the boat.

I saw world-record driver Tommy Harrington throw up his hands in frustration, get out of the boat, and ask another driver to pull the event. This was not just a backyard tournament; it was the U.S. Open. Tommy is a truly great driver. By getting his ego out of the way and allowing a driver who was comfortable with the boat to drive the event, he further proved that he is a skiers' driver.

4. Strive to develop a feel for proper acceleration and throttle control. This will aid both the beginner and the advanced skier. Hold the throttle like an egg. Use your thumb, index finger, and middle finger to hold a constant gentle pressure on the throttle, as shown in figure 2.2.

Figure 2.2   Holding the throttle.

Use your thumb and wrist to control acceleration and the middle finger to control deceleration. Leverage your arm against the gunnel or
arm rest, letting the throttle movement come through the fingers and
wrist, not the arm. The key is to be smooth and consistent with the
throttle.

5. Grip the wheel firmly with the left hand at 10 or 11 o'clock. This
position gives you leverage and control to turn and react to the pull of
the skier. A strong skier will most likely pull the boat around a bit. The
secret is to anticipate the pull and use smooth, controlled adjustments.
Radical, quick, or jerky steering will make things difficult for the skier,
so stay calm and try to work with the skier's rhythm.

6. Keep a straight path by picking a spot on the horizon and driving
to it. This will help you prevent oversteering. Your focus should be
downcourse and your eyes should constantly be scanning the area for
other boats or debris that could hamper the skier.

7. Use the tachometer rather than the speedometer for a more consistent pull. Speedometers will move as the skier pulls the boat. If you
react to the speedometer (which does not respond immediately to

actual speeds) you will have large swings in your speed. By maintaining constant rpm you will respond to the skier's pull in actual time and not have to move the throttle as much. The trick is to learn which rpm reading correlates to a given speed. You will learn this through practice and by taking timed passes.

Driving Patterns

For beginners, a boat pattern that is easy to negotiate is a large loop, usually done in a counterclockwise fashion. This pattern does not require the skier to cross the wakes, and the larger turns prevent the whip effect that can occur when a skier is caught on the outside of the wakes during a turn. If the skier does become caught on the whip the driver should quickly cut back the throttle to prevent the skier from hitting the shore or taking a bad fall.

Once a skier can safely cross the wakes and ski over the boat rollers, a dumbbell pattern is preferred. This pattern (figure 2.3) provides long, straight runs and allows the boat wakes to disperse, leaving the skier with calm water for the next run.

When the skier falls, the driver must do several things to ensure skier safety and keep the water calm for the next run. When the skier goes down, the driver should pull back on the throttle, then turn the steering wheel to the side the skier has fallen and idle around the turn before accelerating back to the skier. This prevents boat rollers from ruining the calm water. Slow the boat well before getting back to the skier and approach the skier on the driver's side of the boat, approximately 15 feet from the skier. Always pass the skier downwind or downcurrent to prevent the possibility of the wind or current pushing the boat into the skier. Make sure the boat is in neutral as you pass the skier. The two ways to pick up a fallen skier are the half-turn method (figure 2.4) and the keyhole method (figure 2.5). Use the method that will take the skier in the direction he or she would like to go.

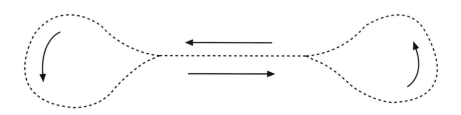

Figure 2.3   The dumbbell driving pattern.

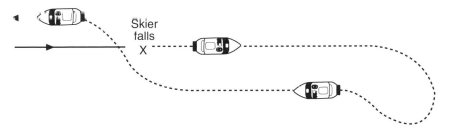

Figure 2.4   The half-turn method to pick up a skier.

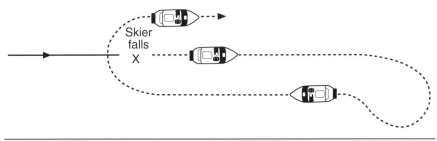

Figure 2.5   The keyhole method to pick up a skier.

Observing

The observer is an essential part of any crew. We recommend that you never ski without an observer, even where state regulations do not require one. The responsibility of the observer is threefold: (1) keep the driver informed of the skier's progress, (2) keep the driver informed of the skier's signals, and (3) assist the driver in being aware of possible safety hazards.

SELECTING A SKI SITE

Every skier's dream is to live on a private ski lake with perfectly sloped banks to prevent backwash and tall trees to keep the wind from disturbing the water. Unfortunately, most of us can't afford this utopian luxury and have to make the best with public lakes and rivers. Luckily, there are numerous public bodies of water that fit the description of the perfect lake rather well. When scouting a ski site for safety and skiability, look for a couple of things. Ideally, you should look for an area 2,000 to 2,400 feet in length and 250 to 300 feet wide. These dimensions allow comfortable setups for the slalom and jump courses and ample room for trick runs. You should always run the boat at least 100 feet from the shore so the skier does not ski into the bank. Although it is possible to ski on shorter bodies of water, you must use caution due to tight setups and turns as well as the need for rapid acceleration.

SELECTING SKI EQUIPMENT

Everyone loves going out to buy the latest and greatest equipment. I remember buying my first slalom ski from Security Sporting Goods in New Orleans. I was in eighth grade, it was springtime, and my parents paid for the ski on the occasion of my confirmation. I promised my mom I would use it religiously. The thought of skiing and teaching professionally never entered my mind. I just wanted to spend all summer on the river cutting up the smooth waters of the Tchefuncte behind our 40-horsepower skiff. The ski was a Stinger Bee, but I don't remember who the manufacturer was. I was lucky; the salesman took time to ask me about my level of ability (beginner), current skis (Dick Pope Jr. combos), and the speed I skied (as fast as the 40-horsepower Johnson would go). Once the salesman knew this he was able to sell me the right ski for my ability, not the one that cost the most or that he had the most of in stock. That guy probably will never know the impact of his honest, insightful salesmanship. You see, by his selling me the right equipment for my size, ability, and speed, I went out and had a great time skiing all summer long. The point is this: Buy the equipment that fits your needs and ability. Too often I see guys and gals busting their butts trying to learn the slalom course on skis that are too small or too advanced for them. They become frustrated and don't have the fun that they paid for when they bought that new high-dollar ski. They would be better off buying the less expensive beginner ski to learn proper technique and position, and later buy the high-end ski. The following is a list of equipment that you will need for water skiing and the characteristics and questions you need to ask your local dealer before laying your money on the counter.

Combo Pairs

These are the basic skis that those just learning to ski most often use. These skis are constructed of wood or fiberglass and have flat or slightly concave bottoms with tapered sides. Adults usually use 60- to 70-inch lengths while children ski on 40- to 50-inch skis. The size you use depends on your weight and the speed you ski. The lighter the person, the smaller the skis. The slower you prefer to ski, the larger your skis should be to reduce drag and fatigue. These types of skis should have adjustable bindings that will come off easily during falls but be well constructed of rubber or a soft synthetic that provides a snug fit with adequate support. Your best bet is to spend the extra few bucks to buy a good fiberglass combo pair with a concave bottom and good-fitting bindings. Fiberglass will last much longer and the bindings will have less chance of ripping due to dry rotting. The real benefit is the slalom ski portion of the pair. This ski has many of the design features of the high-end skis, but slight modifications make it easier to get up on and learn to make smooth, controlled turns. Buying a good combo pair is money well spent given the durability and skiability of the pair.

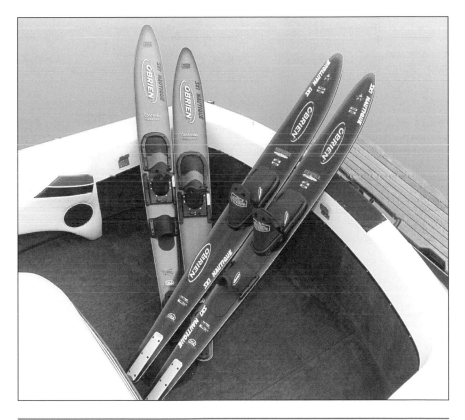

Figure 2.6   Children's combo skis (left) and adult combo skis (right).

Slalom Skis

The manufacturers of water skis go to great pains to match up skis to skiers perfectly. What makes this difficult is that no two skiers are the same, and contrary to popular belief, all slalom skis are not created equal. To get the best ski for you, you must first assess yourself honestly. What is your level of ability? To determine your level of ability, answer the questions in the box below. If you answer yes to three or more statements, you have found your level of ability.

WHAT IS YOUR SLALOM ABILITY?

Entry level:

I have never heard of the slalom course.

I just learned a deep-water start.

I ski once or twice a month.

I ski at boat speeds of 22 to 32 mph.

I am looking for a stable, forgiving, easy-to-ride ski that I can cruise on and get up on easily.

I demand more performance than half a combo set but want an affordable price.

Intermediate to advanced level:

I have tried the slalom course, but mainly ski open water, making huge walls of spray every weekend.

I am just starting to make turns using one hand on the rope or trying to learn how.

I ski at boat speeds between 24 and 34 mph.

I am looking for a more aggressive, faster ski with more holding power out of the turn.

I am not interested in the high-performance trinkets on the ski.

Tournament level:

I ski a slalom course on a regular basis.

I ski at boat speeds of 32 to 36 mph.

I own or ski behind a tournament boat and know what AWSA means.

I enjoy tinkering with and adjusting fins, wings, bindings, flex.

I want and need great acceleration across the wakes and holding power out of the turn.

No matter what your ability, you should look for several things in a slalom ski to make sure it matches your ability and skiing style.

Bottom Design.   We will discuss bottom design in more depth in chapter 5, but for now let's just say a good slalom ski will have a concave bottom. This feature acts like an upside-down airplane wing, sucking the ski to the water. This positive suction allows the ski to hold angle through leans and track better in the turn.

Beveled Edges.   This is the part of the ski that you ride on during the turn. The width and sharpness of the top and bottom edges dictate the turning characteristics of the ski. We cover how to tune these edges in chapter 5.

Rocker.   The greater the rocker, the more the ski will turn but the less it will accelerate. The opposite is true for a flatter ski.

Flex.   The stiffer the ski, the more difficult it is to turn but the better it will accelerate; it's the opposite for a soft ski. A combination of rocker and flex is critical to dialing a ski in to your style. This topic will be covered in chapter 5.

Binding Type and Quality.   Bindings should fit snugly and comfortably. You have several options, adjustable or fixed (also known as plate bindings), and double boots or rear toe piece. Figure 2.7 shows both

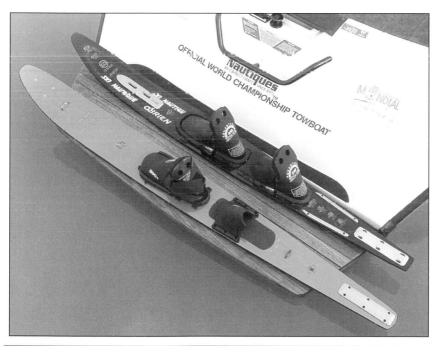

Figure 2.7   Slalom ski binding options: adjustable high-wrap binding with rear toe piece (ski closest to the water) and double high-wrap binding (ski closest to the boat).

combinations. There are advantages to both setups. Let personal preference and comfort guide you. Double boots (ski closest to the boat) offer greater support and secure fit but also cost more. Rear toe piece and adjustable bindings (ski closest to the water) are easier to get up on and get out of but do not give you as good a feel for the ski.

The secret in choosing a slalom ski is not to let your ego or an ignorant salesperson get in the way of your getting the right ski. Select the right ski and you will be off having the best time of your life cutting up the lake rather than fighting the frustrations of falls and body-straining starts. Refer to table 2.1 to determine the correct size ski for you. It is wise to take the time to demo a ski before you spend several hundred bucks. We will provide more technical information on slalom ski design and tuning in chapter 5.

Table 2.1   Slalom Ski Size Guide

| Skier's weight (pounds) | Boat speed (miles per hour) | | | | | |
| | 26 | 28 | 30 | 32 | 34 | 36 |
			(ski size in inches)			
100	64	64	64	64	64	64
100 – 115	66	66	66	64	64	64
115 – 130	67/68	66	66	66	66	66
130 – 145	67/68	67/68	66	66	66	66
145 – 160	67/68	67/68	66	66	66	66
160 – 175	67/68	67/68	67/68	66	66	66/67
175 – 190	69/70	69/70	67/68	67/68	67/68	66/68
190 – 205	69/70	69/70	69/70	67/68	67/68	67/68
205 – 220	69/70	69/70	69/70	69/70	67/68	67/68
220+	69/70	69/70	69/70	69/70	69/70	69/70

Note: If you are on the borderline between sizes, select the larger size ski.

Kneeboards

The top manufacturers offer two types of kneeboards. The traditional rotomolded board, on the right in figure 2.8, is used mainly by recreational skiers and is the least expensive board on the market. The soft, wide edges of rotomolded boards are perfect for beginners and family outings. The smooth turning characteristics of rotomolded boards are still preferred by some of today's top professionals. The compression-molded board, on the left in figure 2.8, offers more performance and durability for the more advanced kneeboarder. They are thinner, lighter, and have sharper edges than rotomolded boards.

Figure 2.8   Compression-molded (left) and rotomolded (right) kneeboards.

Wakeboards

Wakeboards are undergoing a design revolution. Manufacturers are experimenting with new shapes and lighter materials to make the boards easier to edge and turn in the air. Two questions should help you determine which type of wakeboard is best for you.

1. What is your riding style? Do you come from a surfing or water/ snow skiing background, or a snowboarding or skateboarding background? The answer tells you if you should be riding a twin-tip or double-ended board, or a single-tip board. It seems that the single-tip board, on the right in figure 2.9, is preferred by surfers and skiers, while the twin-tip board, on the left in figure 2.9, is the board of choice for snowboarders, trick skiers, and skateboarders.

2. What is your level of ability? The answer determines which type of rails you should look for on a board—square for beginners and round for advanced riders. Similar to slalom skis, an entry-level board needs to track well, be stable, and allow for long cuts outside the wake. A board with a sharp, square rail offers these benefits while keeping the

Figure 2.9   Twin-tip (left) and single-tip (right) wakeboards.

cost down for your first board purchase. The disadvantage to square rails is that they make landings from air tricks more difficult. You have a better chance of catching an edge and taking hard falls with sharp rails. Rounded rails not only make the landings easier and softer but also make tricks easier because you have less chance of catching an edge.

The lightest boards, made with either honeycomb or carbon graphite, offer significant performance enhancements. Some users have broken honeycomb boards, so ask your dealer if the board you want to buy has had this problem and if the manufacturer has remedied it.

Trick Skis

The evolution we are now seeing in wakeboards took place with trick skis in the late 1960s and early 1970s. Manufacturers have now designed skis for the beginner that are easier to ride and adjust to, and skis for the advanced tricker that are lighter and smoother. Trick skis, as seen in figure 2.10, are shorter and wider than normal skis and have no fins. Again, the level of ability is critical in determining which skis are best for you. Numerous well-designed and well-manufactured fiberglass and foam skis offer beginners the stability and tracking they need to learn how to ride tricks. More experienced trickers prefer honeycomb skis because of the lighter weight. In either case, look at several design factors in selecting trick skis.

Edges.   Most trick skis have rounded top edges that allow water to slide over the top of the ski during turns.

Ski Tip Area.   On trick skis, the tip area is similar in design on both the tip and tail—this offers better stability. Whether it is rounded or square is personal preference.

Figure 2.10   Beginning trick skis like these are easier for beginners to ride.

Bottom Design.   The bottom design should be flat, with or without tracking grooves. These grooves help the ski track, but sacrifice rotational speed.

Rocker.   The rocker should run the full length of the ski, or there should be a short flat spot in the center of the ski with gradual rocker over the remainder of the ski. This rocker pattern makes surface tricks smoother and edging the ski easier.

Weight.   Skis should be as light as possible for easy turns and better control.

Length.   The skier should match length with his or her weight according to table 2.2.

Jumpers

The physical demands of jumping are considerable. Designers and manufacturers of jumpers know this and have designed jumpers for every talent level. Whether you are a beginner or a 200-plus jumper, it is imperative that you get jump skis that are safe, durable, and fit your size and skill level. As with trick skis, jumpers are made of either fiberglass/foam for beginners and less aggressive jumpers or honeycomb and graphite for serious jumpers. No matter which material is used, you should look at several performance characteristics before buying any set of jumpers.

Ski Tip.   On jumpers, the ski tip should be wider than the middle of the ski, or at least the same width, to create lift in the air.

Table 2.2   Trick Ski Size Guide

Weight (pounds)	Size (inches)
0 – 80	36 – 38
80 – 120	38 – 40
120 – 160	40 – 42
160 – 180	42 – 44
180+	44

Note: Divisions between sizes are approximate. Seek the advice of a coach to assist you in your choice.

Edges. Jumpers have flat edges on both the top and bottom to promote faster turns and hold angle better.

Bottom Design. Bottoms must be smooth to give full acceleration during cuts.

Rocker. The rocker should be moderate from tip to tail and aid in the turning and stability of the skis.

Flex. Flex should be softer for beginners and lighter jumpers and stiffer for more advanced and heavier jumpers.

Fins. Fins should be made of a strong material such as plastic.

Length. Skiers should match the length of the skis to their body weight as shown in table 2.3. This sizing table is for less experienced jumpers who are jumping less than 100 feet. The more serious jumpers are now riding longer skis to create more lift and float in the air. Skiers must use caution when making the switch to the longer skis. We will discuss this, along with the details of jump skis and jumping equipment, in greater detail in chapter 7.

Table 2.3   Novice Skier Jump Ski Size Guide

Weight (pounds)	Size (inches)
90 – 110	65 – 67
110 – 140	67 – 70
140 – 180	70 – 72
180+	73 – 74

Note: Divisions between sizes are approximate. Seek the advice of a coach to assist you in your choice.

Accessories

When selecting accessories for skiing, value is the operative word. Here are a few things to consider.

Ropes. If you're just starting out, buy an eight-loop slalom rope as seen in the front of figure 2.11. Buy an 80-strand rope rather than a 60-strand rope—it will last longer and is safer. Get a rope made by a reputable manufacturer so you know the cutoff loops measure correctly and the rope is of high quality. A slalom rope with cutoff loops is the only choice for a serious slalom skier, but you can also use it for casual

Figure 2.11   Ropes. An eight-loop slalom rope (front of photo) is a good all-purpose rope that can be adjusted for tricking and boarding. As you advance, you can move to a 70-foot jump line (top right) or a trick line (top left).

skiing and learning to jump. It's easy to adjust for tricking or boarding, too. As you advance, consider buying a 70-foot jump line (top right in photo) or a trick line (top left in photo).

Handle.   If you are simply slalom skiing or jumping, buy a handle similar to the one shown on the left in figure 2.12. It should be easy to grip and hold on to, but not so hard that it will tear or rip your hands. A coated bridle is preferred for safety. If you are a big-time boarder, the center handle in the photo is your best bet. The extra weaving of the rope makes body-wrap tricks easier and safer. If you're a trick skier, you also want a rope with extra weaving. Trickers need a special handle so they can perform toe tricks. The toe-hold harness, as shown by the right handle in the photo, should be tight yet comfortable and have protective wrapping, weaving, and coating on the bridle.

Protective Gear.   Figures 2.13 and 2.14 show some of the gear you must buy, and some you *should* buy, before you hit the water.

- Gloves. Try on several pairs and look for features such as double-stitched seams, padded or Kevlar palms, and tight wrist straps that prevent the gloves from sliding up your hand (figure 2.13a).
- Glove liners. You may want to consider glove liners or protectors (figure 2.13b) if you plan to spend lots of time on the water. They will permit you to ski longer and have more fun.

Figure 2.12   Handles. The slalom handle on the left can also be used as an all-purpose handle. Handles for boarding (center) and tricking (right) have extra weaving to make body-wrap tricks easier. The trick handle also has a toe-hold harness for toe tricks.

- Back braces (figure 2.13c), leg protectors (figure 2.13d), and skiing shorts (figure 2.13e). Use these items if you have special needs or problems, or if you feel more comfortable with them. The choice is yours.
- Life vest. Your vest should be a USCG-approved personal flotation device (PFD) with four or five buckles (figure 2.13f). Nonapproved tournament vests are lighter and more comfortable (figure 2.13g), but you should use these only in controlled environments or tournaments. These vests do not count as PFDs when the Coast Guard checks you.
- Wet suits. The first thing you should determine is what you will be doing in your wet suit. If you are jumping, spend the money to buy a quality jump suit that will withstand the impact of jumping (far right in figure 2.14). For winter skiing, get a full suit or a dry suit, shown second from the left in the photo. The best value for my buck is a three-quarter suit shown second from the left in the photo. This suit is warm but still light and more flexible than a full or dry suit. A shorty, shown on the far left, is ideal for cooler days or to help keep the morning chill off. The secret is to buy the right suit for your type of skiing.

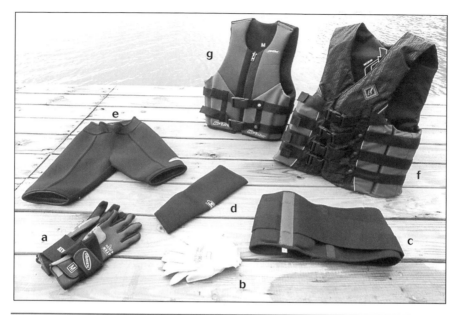

Figure 2.13   Protective gear: (a) gloves; (b) glove liners; (c) back brace; (d) leg protector; (e) skiing shorts; (f) USCG-approved life vest; (g) tournament vest.

Figure 2.14   Wet suits. Shorty (far left), three-quarter suit (second from left), dry suit (second from right), and jump suit (far right).

- Sun gear. A final consideration is protecting yourself from the sun. A good, full hat and sunscreen are a must, as are quality sunglasses. You may want to throw in some soap or binding slime to save on wear and tear on your bindings and some type of muscle ache cream just in case.

CHOOSING THE BOAT FOR YOU

You can ski behind almost anything—fishing boats, runabouts, skiffs, even personal watercraft. The minimum power requirement to pull an adult is in the 50- to 100-horsepower range, depending on your size. But if you are looking for a great family boat that provides plenty of room and excellent dependability, as well as ideal skiing characteristics, look no further than the inboards on the market today. Manufacturers such as Nautiques by Correct Craft are offering boats that perform and handle better than the best outboards and stern drives on the market. The inboards of today are no longer just for tournament skiers; they combine the best skiing qualities with roominess for entire families and the ease of maintenance for which inboards are famous. As with any purchase, you want the best value for your dollar. Take a good look at the new inboards and compare them to the outboards and stern drives before you buy a boat. In every price range you will find one that fits exactly what you are looking for. The important thing is to get on the water, no matter what your type of power. Let's check out the things you should look for in making your buying decision.

Handling

A ski boat should be responsive, have little or no dead rise, and should plane off quickly. (Dead rise is the amount the bow lifts when you take off out of the hole.) Once on plane the boat should be able to hold a constant speed, even at lower speeds of 12 to 18 mph for tricking, and be able to maintain a straight path, even with a skier pulling on the rope. Maintaining a constant lower speed is a major problem for outboards and stern drives and makes pulling children, lighter skiers, or trickers extremely difficult. The driver should not have to fight the wheel to get the boat to track straight, especially in the slalom course. The boat should be able to corner without heeling over on its side and have excellent maneuverability at slow speeds.

Wakes

Wakes can be a major stumbling block for beginners and smaller, lighter skiers. The wakes for slalom and jump should be as small as possible with a minimum rooster tail between them. For tricking, and boarding at speeds of 12 to 20 mph, the wakes should be clean and crisp with a sharp rise and flat table behind the boat.

Visibility

A low dead rise contributes to both easy handling and good visibility. The driver should always be able to see everything in front of the boat. The windshield must not obstruct the driver's view and should be fitted with a rearview mirror.

Controls and Gauges

The steering and throttle need to be smooth and easy to control from the driver's seat, with a forearm rest for comfort and driveability. The boat should be fitted with two speedometers and standard running gauges such as oil, battery, temperature, and fuel.

Tow Pylon

Ideally, a tow pylon is located in the middle of the boat in front of the engine. In outboards and stern drives this is usually not possible, so a rear pylon is used. This type of pylon allows the skier to move the boat

Figure 2.15   Let's hit the water!

and makes it difficult for the driver to steer. Because of the steering difficulties and location of a rear pylon near the engine, use caution and make sure the rope does not become tangled in the prop.

Buying a ski boat is not only a financial investment but an investment in fun. Select one constructed with high-quality, durable materials. Read the warranties and learn about maintenance.

Now we're ready. We have all the latest and best gear, a top-quality ski boat, and the family is loaded up. Let's hit the water.

WATER SKIING FITNESS

Most skiers, even some of the best-known pros, train haphazardly. They decide what they'll do as they get into the water, or worse, let the whims of others determine their intensity level. Many skiers become caught up in what I call the ski culture. They train based on lore accumulated over the years from famous skiers but do not know how to use recent scientific advances in the four elements of a complete training program: fitness, nutrition, on-water training, and mental toughness. In this chapter we will reveal the latest information on two of the four key elements of peak performance—fitness and nutrition. We will cover the other two essential elements, on-water training and mental toughness, in later chapters. By incorporating a fitness and nutrition plan into your training, you will feel better physically and have more confidence and energy in your skiing.

FIVE FOR FITNESS

A complete skiing fitness program includes five essential components. The following is a synopsis of the scientific data behind each element and a fitness program designed for every level of skier from the weekend warrior to the aspiring champion.

Abdominal Training

Your abdominals and obliques (the muscles on the side of your abdominals) represent the core of all strength. Weak abdominals and poor fitness are synonymous with each other. Low-back pain, poor posture, inflexibility, and breathing problems can all be linked to abdominal weakness. These are all common problems for water skiers, so strong abs are a must. A weakness in your core of strength can predispose you to injury and undermine the hours you spend trying to toughen up physically. James Lorhr, EdD recommends a minimum of 200 curl-ups or modified sit-ups each day for athletes in training. That may seem excessive, but the abs are that important in skiing. Testing performed on pro skiers at the Olympic Training Center has shown that top skiers have extremely strong abs. Start easy and build up to the recommended 200 reps a day, but get those abs strong if you want to improve.

Cardiovascular Training

How much cardiorespiratory stress you should expose yourself to is determined by the event you wish to excel in. The key is that you challenge and train your heart and lungs to meet the physical, mental, and emotional energy requirements of your event. Nothing is more

Figure 3.1   Strong abs are a must for doing tricks like this.

demoralizing than huffing and puffing as the rope tightens up for your most difficult slalom pass.

In slalom you typically have 20 to 30 seconds of all-out activity that raises the heart rate, followed by a similar rest period for recovery. In jumping, however, testing has shown that the heart rate rises when the skier leaves the dock and does not decrease until he or she lands after the last jump. These differences are important because you should train for competition situations. During competition you use your heart and lung capacity almost twice as quickly as you do during practice, so you must train for this extra oxygen requirement. You will be amazed at the confidence boost you get when the rope tightens up and your breathing is calm and comfortable. You feel strong and energized, ready to take on the course, the boat, and anything that may get between you and your goals.

Since water skiing is an anaerobic activity, the largest portion of your cardiorespiratory training will consist of activities that are specific to anaerobic conditioning, such as interval or circuit training. Cross-country skiing, stair climbing, in-line skating, rowing, cycling, and running are all excellent methods of improving cardiorespiratory conditioning. The secret is to perform them at the recommended volumes and intensities. To do high-intensity interval training, you must have a general fitness level that will tolerate the stress placed on the body. We will develop this general fitness by improving our aerobic conditioning.

Aerobic Training.   Aerobic (meaning with oxygen) conditioning is performed by sustaining low-intensity exercise for long periods 70 to 85 percent of heart rate reserve (refer to the box on page 34) for 30 to 90 minutes. Recent studies recommend exercise that involves both upper and lower body movement, for example, jogging or cross-country skiing simulators. A 4- to 5-mile jog, a 10- to 20-mile bike ride, or a workout on a cross-country skiing simulator three to five times a week is ideal. Aerobic training is used primarily in the off-season to build a solid fitness foundation before beginning more strenuous on-water training. Aerobic training also has benefits during the ski season; aerobic fitness will aid in rapid muscular recovery during competition.

Anaerobic (Interval or Circuit) Training.   Anaerobic (meaning without oxygen) conditioning, also known as interval or circuit training, is performed by doing high-intensity work for a shorter period—85 to 95 percent of heart rate reserve for one to three minutes followed by a short rest and another period of exercise. The goal of this type of training is to stress the anaerobic system to its maximum limit in a repetitive cycle with a fixed work-rest ratio. Due to the repetition, the aerobic system gets a good workout as well. The work-rest relationship should

DETERMINING YOUR HEART RATE RESERVE (HRR)

This procedure will help you determine your heart rate reserve. It accounts for relative differences in resting heart rate (HR).

HRR = [(220 − your age) − (resting HR)] × % workload + (resting HR)

For example, suppose you are 20 years old with a resting heart rate of 60 and you want to estimate your heart rate at 70 percent of your maximum:

$$\begin{aligned} HRR &= [(220 - 20) - 60] \times .7 + 60 \\ &= 140 \times .7 + 60 \\ &= 98 + 60 \\ &= 158 \text{ beats per minute} \end{aligned}$$

Take your heart rate before, during, and after training. Count your pulse for 10 seconds and multiply by six to calculate heart rate. Always take your heart rate at the end of a high-intensity interval.

be 90 seconds of work and 30 seconds of rest for interval training. The HRR should be 85 to 95 percent during the work stages and 70 to 75 percent during rest periods. Examples of interval training would be 4 3 400-meter runs (90 seconds) or 4 3 800-meter bike sprints, with a slow jog or bike pace (30 seconds) between work stages at 75 percent HRR, done two to four times a week. Circuit training combines a strength workout with one-minute aerobic exercise to keep the heart rate at high levels between exercises. Perform these sessions during the preseason and into the competitive season, when intensity peaks.

Strength Development

Depending on the demands of your event, you should regularly overload your muscles with stress to increase overall strength. Terry Eberhardt, chairman of the American Water Ski Association (AWSA) Sports Medicine/Sports Science Committee, emphasizes three key principles that you should understand about resistance training: overload, specificity, and reversibility.

Overload Principle.   The overload principle says that to increase the physical capacity of muscles, you must progressively exercise the muscles at a level above what they ordinarily do. There are three variables of the overload principle: frequency, intensity, and time (FIT). Frequency refers to the number of days a specific exercise is performed per week. Intensity refers to the workload at which the exercise is performed. Time refers to the amount of time spent performing the exercises. A successful training program must include all three overload variables. The overload principle, which applies to both on- and off-water training, must be balanced carefully to avoid overtraining. We will discuss overtraining and rest in depth later in this chapter.

Specificity Principle.   The principle of specificity refers to the type of adaptation that takes place as a direct result of training. The development of muscles is specific to the type of stress placed upon those muscles. Strength and conditioning training programs should stress the muscles used during the sport or activity. Although there is a carryover from one type of training to another, it is not enough to improve performance significantly. Knowing this, it becomes important to develop on- and off-water training programs specific to your competitive event or desired area of improvement. An example of this would be in slalom, where the muscles in the abdomen (rectus abdominis), back (latissimus dorsi), buttocks (gluteus maximus), front of the thigh (quadriceps), and forearms (forearm flexors) are used with high intensity. It would be wise to give these muscle groups specific attention when doing resistance training.

Reversibility Principle.   The principle of reversibility is the principle underlying the common saying "Use it or lose it." Gains will be lost if overload is not continued. Fitness is lost twice as fast as it is gained. It is important to incorporate resistance training and aerobic conditioning into your in-season training program to maintain the fitness level gained in the off-season. Research has shown that you can maintain strength and conditioning gains by training as infrequently as once a week, as long as the intensity of training is sufficient to incite overload.

The objective of resistance training is to increase the strength of muscles and other soft tissue (ligaments, tendons) to improve performance and prevent injury. Resistance training programs should emphasize strengthening muscles that are specific to the physical task—skiing—and should progressively overload these muscles.

Free-weight exercises are the traditional choice because they allow for better development of neuromotor coordination and specific strengthening along the movement patterns used in skiing. Variable resistance machines, or other cam systems, allow equal strengthening over a full range of motion and better isolation of the muscles involved. An additional benefit of variable resistance machines is that a higher intensity of training can be attained by isolating muscles and working

PLYOMETRIC EXERCISES

STEP-UPS:

Start with a step 6 to 12 inches high. Step onto the step, planting the entire foot on it. Bring both feet onto the step, then step off one leg at a time. Repeat with the other foot. Start by exercising for 30 seconds and increase as you adapt to the exercise.

SIDE JUMPS:

Jump laterally (sideways) over a barrier such as a cone or rope. You can start with a rope about three inches high. You should explode into the next jump once the feet land on one side of the barrier. Increase speed and time as you improve.

them to complete exhaustion. Research recommends a combination of both types of resistance training. You should change the volume and intensity of training throughout the year to reach peak performance for certain events and avoid overtraining. To achieve this balance, use periodization of your training schedule. The strength-training program provided in this chapter is periodized for a peak during the main summer months. We provide more information on this important training concept in chapter 10.

A second form of strength development that is beneficial to water skiers is plyometrics. The use of plyometric exercises for sports that require agility and explosive movement is nothing new. Athletes in

BOUNDING:

Use either one or two legs. Push off and jump as high and as far as you possibly can. Upon landing, jump explosively up and forward with a strong arm swing. To keep yourself working hard, set out a series of blocks or obstacles to clear along your path. Increase your yardage and time as you adapt to the exercise.

LUNGES:

Stand with both feet together. Step forward with one leg until that leg makes a 90-degree angle with the floor. Keep the opposite leg straight. Push off explosively with the forward leg returning to the starting position. Repeat with the opposite leg.

Reprinted, by permission, from D.A. Chu, 1992, *Jumping into Plyometrics* (Champaign, IL: Human Kinetics).

basketball, football, track and field, volleyball, and snow skiing have successfully used plyometrics to improve speed, quickness, reaction time, and jumping ability. The forces imposed on the skier by the boat, rope, wakes, and skis require rapid and powerful response. Biomechanical analysis has shown that plyometrics can improve the skier's movements. The primary objective is to increase the excitability of the nervous system for improved reactive ability of the neuromuscular system. Improving the functioning of the neuromuscular system will produce quicker and more explosive movements. One plyometric exercise you're already familiar with is jumping rope. Other examples of this type of training are shown in the box above.

Products such as Strength Shoes can also be beneficial in performing plyometrics. These shoes create added stress on the calf muscles and stretch the Achilles tendon by elevating the ball of the foot. By lifting the forefoot, the calf and Achilles support the entire weight of the body, thereby overloading the area.

Exercise caution when performing plyometrics. When performed correctly the results can be incredible; however, when overused or used incorrectly plyometrics can ruin an athlete's season or career due to the extreme stress placed on the body. It is important that any athlete who begins a plyometrics training program start by developing a strength base. To be able to perform the exercises for the later phases, you will need a solid foundation.

Progressive Injury Care

How many times have you been forced to sit out or stay home because of the same bad knee or weak shoulder? When you have an injury you lose confidence in the area injured, and the natural instinct is to protect it. Since the injury can't take as much stress we don't push it. This is why the injury recurs. To rebuild confidence following injury, use a three-step procedure:

Figure 3.2   Plyometrics can help improve your ability to perform explosive movements like those required for jumping.

1. Protect the injured limb, joint, or muscle from stress immediately following the breakdown. Use the PRICE method. First you **Pro**tect and **R**est the injured area. Put **I**ce on the injured area as soon as possible. Next use **C**ompression (apply pressure to the area); then you **E**levate the injury. This method will prevent swelling, and you should start it immediately.
2. Expose the injured area to progressively increasing stress as soon as the injury has stabilized. Start with light stretching and build from there.
3. Continue to do the rehabilitation exercises even after the injured limb is as strong as the healthy limb.

Active Stretching

Injuries can affect confidence mightily. Muscle flexibility plays a critical role in any injury prevention program. A new generation of stretching, developed by kinesiologist Aaron L. Mattes, is receiving fantastic reviews from professional skiers and Olympic athletes as well as medical professionals.

The purpose of stretching is to increase flexibility, relieve muscle soreness, prevent injury, warm up and cool down muscles, provide greater potential for athletic skills, and aid in recovery from injury. The key to Mattes's unprecedented success in improving the range of motion and reducing and preventing injuries in his patients is a basic understanding of muscle physiology.

The earliest form of stretching, called ballistic stretching, was abandoned several decades ago. Athletes who tried it found that the rapid bouncing into and out of positions caused muscle soreness and sometimes even muscle tears. The second generation of stretching was "static" stretching. This static method, which advocates holding a position for 30 to 60 seconds, reached mass popularity through numerous books and articles. Since static stretching involves no rapid movements, proponents argued, it should promote flexibility without producing soreness, through gradual adaptation to the stretch. However, static stretching produces more soreness and higher levels of creatine kinase, an enzyme associated with muscle-tissue injury, than does ballistic stretching.

Why do these methods of stretching create problems? Basic muscle physiology teaches us that all muscles have a "stretch reflex" that is activated after a strong, rapid movement or after two seconds on a stretched position. The stretch reflex causes the muscle to begin a slow contraction. Continuing to stretch while your muscle is trying to contract can cause muscle damage.

TEN WATER SKIERS' STRETCHES

Neck lateral flexion: Standing straight, press your ear to your shoulder by contracting cervical flexors and assisting with your hand. Perform this stretch on both sides of your neck for 8 to 10 repetitions.

Horizontal shoulder flexion: To stretch the external shoulder rotators, place your left arm level with your shoulders, and reach around your right arm midway between the shoulders and pectoralis (chest). Place your right hand on your left elbow to assist the stretch at the end of the movement. Do this stretch for both arms for 8 to 10 repetitions.

Neck rotation: Rotate your chin to your shoulder, assisting with your hand placed on your jaw. Do 8 to 10 stretches and repeat on the opposite side.

Horizontal abduction: To stretch the pectoralis (chest), place your wrist against a post or wall with palm forward and at shoulder height. Rotate or move forward away from the support and stretch 6 to 8 repetitions on each side.

(continued)

Single-leg pelvic tilt: This stretch is for the lower back and gluteus maximus. Flex your left knee and pull it toward your chest, contracting the hip flexor and abdominal muscles. Place your hands behind the thigh to provide assistance at the end of the free movement. Repeat with the opposite leg. Perform 10 or more repetitions.

Rectus femoris (quadriceps): This stretch is for the lower hip and quads. Place your hand under your right foot to stabilize the leg. Flex your left leg and grab the ankle. Contract the abdominal muscles to prevent forward tilt of the pelvis. Maintain upper leg in flexed position throughout movement. Contract gluteus maximus and hamstrings, reaching backward with the hand to give gentle assistance. Do two sets of 10 with alternating legs.

Hamstrings: This muscle is stretched by a constant contraction of the quadriceps. Do not allow the leg to bend at any point in the movement. Lift the leg slowly with the quadriceps. Give gentle assistance with a rope or hands at the end of the movement Do two sets of 10, alternating legs after each set.

Trunk flexion: Begin from an upright sitting position. Exhale, tuck chin, flex knees two to three inches, and contract abdominals strongly as body curls forward. Do not bounce or move rapidly at the end of the stretch. Use the hands to pull yourself forward at the end of the stretch. Perform 10 to 15 repetitions.

(continued)

Trunk rotation: This stretch is for thoracic and lumbar rotators. Sit with your left leg straight. Flex your right knee 90 degrees and cross over and rest to the outside knee. Place your left elbow on the outside of flexed knee. Rest your right hand behind your back. Turn head and trunk as far as possible away from midline and assist with elbow pressure against knee. Do 8 to 10 repetitions.

Achilles tendon/calf: Bring the knee into the chest and grab the foot below the toes. Stretch the calf and Achilles by flexing the ankle-foot dorsal flexor muscles toward the knee. Use the hands to assist the stretch. Do 8 to 10 repetitions on each foot.

Mattes has spent over 65,000 hours studying, developing, practicing, and instructing a third generation of stretching called active isolated (AI) stretching. In AI stretching, you hold each position for only 1 ½ to 2 seconds. Then you return to the starting position and relax. After resting for 2 seconds, you ease into the stretch again exhaling with each stretch. AI stretching differs from static stretching in ways beyond the 2-second limitation. In AI stretching, stretches are "assisted" in two ways. First, you contract the opposing muscle group to help move the stretched area into position. Second, while continuing the contraction, you use a rope or your hands gently to enhance the stretch. The cardinal rule of stretching remains unchanged: Don't ever force yourself beyond the point of light irritation.

Stretching is never an instant solution to an injury problem, so take your time. The best results come from consistent, gentle stretching. AI stretching is great, but you must find what works best for you and keep working on improving your flexibility. Try incorporating into your training routine the preceding stretches. Aaron Mattes himself has selected these stretches as those most likely to help skiers increase flexibility and prevent injuries. Hold each stretch for 1 ½ to 2 seconds.

SAMPLE FITNESS PROGRAMS

An overview of two fitness programs follows—one for weekend skiers and one for competitive skiers. They'll help build the strength and cardiovascular fitness you need to take your skiing to the next level.

Setting a Baseline for Fitness

Before beginning, you should ascertain your starting level of fitness. Doing so will allow you to set goals and measure improvement. Critical information includes accurate measurement of height, weight, and body fat percentage. Your local gym or doctor can provide this for you.

In addition, do as many pull-ups and sit-ups as you can in one minute. You'll use this to determine how many repetitions you'll complete during training sessions.

Warming Up

It is essential to do a proper warm-up before each workout and even more important to do a complete cool-down afterward. The purpose of a warm-up is to assist the body in making the transition from rest to exercise. The objective is to increase the blood flow to the working skeletal muscles and raise the tissue temperature. Increased blood flow increases the amount of oxygen available to the muscles for contractions. The increased muscle temperature increases the joint range of motion and allows nerve impulses to travel faster, enhancing the speed of muscle contractions and reaction time. Your warm-up should begin with 5 to 10 minutes of light aerobic activity (biking, jogging) followed by a stretching and flexibility routine. Research has shown that a properly conducted warm-up can reduce the risk of injuries.

Cooling Down

Although often forgotten, the cool-down is an extremely important component of a training program. The cool-down consists of light exercise following a training session. A slow bike ride or jog followed by stretching is ideal. The objective is to return all metabolic functions gradually to preexercise levels. The cool-down also aids in reducing soreness by speeding the removal of lactic acid and other cellular waste from the muscles. The cool-down should last for 5 to 10 minutes.

Setting a Baseline for Strength

The strength-training exercises in the sample programs are organized to work each major muscle group with one or two exercises. Add additional exercises as desired or if you notice specific weaknesses. Consult a weight-training book to learn how to do these exercises properly, or ask qualified personnel at a fitness facility.

Before you do any strength-training exercises, determine your one-repetition maximum (1RM) for bench press and squats. Do this by first loosening up and then going for broke. Lift as much weight as you can for one repetition. If you have never done a 1RM, ask a qualified fitness instructor to help you. If you have done a 1RM, remember to use a spotter so you don't get hurt.

Here are 10 tips to help you get the most benefit from the program:

1. Use common sense. Your schedule should fit your needs. Consider work, school, and other activities. Listen to your body, and get rest.
2. Vary the workouts. Use the program that fits your needs. You may alter the program to suit your strengths and weaknesses.
3. Accentuate the lowering portion of each repetition.
4. Never increase the weight or time by more than 5 percent of the previous workout.
5. Always include a 10-minute warm-up and cool-down.
6. Always stretch during your warm-up and cool-down.

7. Work large muscles first.
8. Include a good flexibility program and diet to go along with your strength and cardiovascular training.
9. Do not sacrifice form in an attempt to lift more weight.
10. Do your cardiovascular workout after your strength workout.

Your goal for fitness training is to develop a body for water skiing. Too many skiers adopt strength programs that are great for body builders or football players, athletes who need bodies exactly opposite than needed for skiing. A skier's body needs to be strong and lean, not bulky. Your strength-to-weight ratio needs to be high. Look at Andy Mapple—you don't see a bulky, strapping ox, you see a lean, strong, quick greyhound. The recommended training programs will help you accomplish this goal. Don't take the weekend warrior program lightly. It is slightly less intense than the competitive program but will require dedication and time to make gains. The competitive skier program and schedule is for the serious skier and should be monitored carefully. The competitive program is scheduled out for the entire season, or periodized, into four phases for maximum gains and to prevent overtraining. We provide more information on periodization in chapter 10.

OVERTRAINING

To improve your skiing, you must train longer, harder, and more frequently. That's fine except for one little problem. How do you know when you have overdone it and become a victim of overtraining? It is not easy to determine exactly how much training your body can handle. If you can't figure this out, and most cannot, you risk chronic fatigue, injuries, and poor performances—exactly the opposite of what those hours of hard training are supposed to achieve. Worse yet, your subpar performances may continue for weeks or even months. That's the bad news. The good news is that exercise scientists are developing techniques to help athletes detect and avoid overtraining and the syndrome of symptoms it presents.

Successful development of an athlete is always a delicate balancing act between three variables: a training program of progressive overload, the correct raw materials (nutrients) to maintain and repair tissue and build new tissue, and sufficient rest and sleep (7+ to 9+ hours of sleep a night as a rule) to permit the repair and new growth to take place. Olympian Jeff Galloway put it best: "The single greatest cause of improvement is remaining injury-free to train." And the best insurance against injury is knowing when and when not to train so you avoid overtraining.

Weekend Warrior Strength and Conditioning Program

If you are a weekend skier and want to get in shape to have more fun on the water, this is the program for you. This is a great general fitness program that will help you in everything you do. To gauge the amount of weight to lift in weight training exercises, use this rule: If you can do 15 repetitions, add weight; if you can't do 10, reduce weight.

MONDAY

Warm-up	10-15 minutes
Sit-ups	3 × maximum number you can complete
Plyometric drills	
Jump rope	2-5 minutes
Step-ups	1 minute
Side jumps	1 minute
Cool-down	10-15 minutes

TUESDAY

Warm-up	10-15 minutes
Squats or leg press	2 × 10-15 repetitions
Leg curls	1 × 10-15 repetitions
Leg extensions	1 × 10-15 repetitions
Aerobic conditioning	20-40 minutes
Cool-down	10-15 minutes

WEDNESDAY

Same as Monday

THURSDAY

Warm-up	10-15 minutes
Bench press	1 × 10-15 repetitions
Military press	1 × 10-15 repetitions
Lat pull down	1 × 10-15 repetitions
Arm curls	1 × 10-15 repetitions
Triceps extensions	1 × 10-15 repetitions
Back extensions	1 × 10-15 repetitions
Aerobic conditioning	20-40 minutes
Cool-down	10-15 minutes

FRIDAY

Same as Monday

Competition Skier Strength and Conditioning Program

We have designed this program for the skier who wants to compete on an amateur or professional level. The program is based on data accumulated by testing top pro skiers at the Olympic Training Center. This program offers incredible total body fitness. It does not consider your skiing schedule and other demands, so you must use your judgment to refine the program to fit your specific need and overcome your weaknesses. Please note that *rest* on rest days means complete and total rest. No skiing. Your only activity on these days should be sleep and light stretching.

Preparation Period January 1–February 15: Perform strength-training exercises at 65 percent of your one-repetition maximum. Perform aerobic training at 75 percent of your HRR. Perform anaerobic training at 85 percent of your HRR.

MONDAY

	Week 1-2	Week 3-4	Week 5-6
Warm-up	10-15 minutes	10-15 minutes	10-15 minutes
Sit-ups	3 × max	3 × max	3 × max
Squats or leg press	3-5 × 10-15	3-5 × 10-15	1 × max
Leg curls	2 × 10-15	2 × 10-15	1 × max
Squats or leg press	2 × 10-15	2 × 10-15	2 × 10-15
Leg curls	2 × 10-15	2 × 10-15	2 × 10-15
Leg extensions	2 × 10-15	2 × 10-15	2 × 10-15
Bench press	2 × 10-15	2 × 10-15	2 × 10-15
Military press	2 × 10-15	2 × 10-15	2 × 10-15
Lat pull down	2 × 10-15	2 × 10-15	2 × 10-15
Arm curls	2 × 10-15	2 × 10-15	2 × 10-15
Triceps extensions	2 × 10-15	2 × 10-15	2 × 10-15
Back extensions	2 × 10-15	2 × 10-15	2 × 10-15
Leg extensions	2 × 10-15	2 × 10-15	2 × 10-15
Bench press	2 × 10-15	2 × 10-15	2 × 10-15
Military press	2 × 10-15	2 × 10-15	2 × 10-15
Lat pull down	2 × 10-15	2 × 10-15	2 × 10-15
Arm curls	2 × 10-15	2 × 10-15	2 × 10-15
Triceps extensions	2 × 10-15	2 × 10-15	2 × 10-15
Back extensions	2 × 10-15	2 × 10-15	2 × 10-15
Cool-down	10-15 minutes	10-15 minutes	10-15 minutes

TUESDAY

	Week 1-2	Week 3-4	Week 5-6
Warm-up	10-15 minutes	10-15 minutes	10-15 minutes
Interval training	4-7 intervals	4-7 intervals	4-7 intervals

Plyometric training

Jump rope	5-10 minutes	5-10 minutes	5-10 minutes
Step-ups	2-4 minutes	2-4 minutes	2-4 minutes
Side jumps	2-4 minutes	2-4 minutes	2-4 minutes
Cool-down	10-15 minutes	10-15 minutes	10-15 minutes

WEDNESDAY

	Week 1-2	Week 3-4	Week 5-6
Warm-up	10-15 minutes	10-15 minutes	10-15 minutes

Circuit training

Perform 1 minute aerobic exercise immediately following each strength exercise:

Squats or leg press	1 × 10-15	1 × 10-15	1 × 8-10
Leg curls	1 × 10-15	1 × 10-15	1 × 10-15
Leg extensions	1 × 10-15	1 × 10-15	1 × 10-15
Bench press	1 × 10-15	1 × 10-15	1 × 10-15
Military press	1 × 10-15	1 × 10-15	1 × 10-15
Lat pull down	1 × 10-15	1 × 10-15	1 × 10-15
Arm curls	1 × 10-15	1 × 10-15	1 × 10-15
Triceps extensions	1 × 10-15	1 × 10-15	1 × 10-15
Back extensions	1 × 10-15	1 × 10-15	1 × 10-15

Plyometric training

Jump rope	5-10 minutes	5-10 minutes	5-10 minutes
Bounding	2-4 minutes	2-4 minutes	2-4 minutes
Side jumps	2-4 minutes	2-4 minutes	2-4 minutes
Cool-down	10-15 minutes	10-15 minutes	10-15 minutes

THURSDAY

Rest

FRIDAY

Warm-up	10-15 minutes	10-15 minutes	10-15 minutes

Repeat strength-training exercises from Monday

Interval training	3-6 intervals	3-6 intervals	3-6 intervals
Cool-down	10-15 minutes	10-15 minutes	10-15 minutes

SATURDAY

Rest

SUNDAY

Rest

Precompetitive Period February 22–April 7: Perform strength training at 80 percent of your one-repetition maximum. Perform aerobic training at 70 percent of your HRR. Perform anaerobic training at 90 percent of your HRR.

MONDAY

	Week 1-2	Week 3-4	Week 5-6
Warm-up	10-15 minutes	10-15 minutes	10-15 minutes
Circuit training			
Perform 1 minute aerobic exercise immediately following each strength exercise:			
Squats or leg press	2 × 10-15	2 × 10-15	2 × 10-15
Leg curls	1 × 10-15	1 × 10-15	1 × 10-15
Leg extensions	1 × 10-15	1 × 10-15	1 × 10-15
Bench press	1 × 10-15	1 × 10-15	1 × 10-15
Military press	1 × 10-15	1 × 10-15	1 × 10-15
Lat pull down	1 × 10-15	1 × 10-15	1 × 10-15
Arm curls	1 × 10-15	1 × 10-15	1 × 10-15
Triceps extensions	1 × 10-15	1 × 10-15	1 × 10-15
Back extensions	1 × 10-15	1 × 10-15	1 × 10-15
Sit-ups	4 × max	4 × max	4 × max
Cool-down	10-15 minutes	10-15 minutes	10-15 minutes

TUESDAY

Warm-up	10-15 minutes	10-15 minutes	10-15 minutes
Interval training	6-10 intervals	6-10 intervals	6-10 intervals
Plyometric training			
Jump rope	5-10 minutes	5-10 minutes	5-10 minutes
Step-ups	2-4 minutes	2-4 minutes	2-4 minutes
Side jumps	2-4 minutes	2-4 minutes	2-4 minutes
Lunges	2-4 minutes	2-4 minutes	2-4 minutes
Bounding	2-4 minutes	2-4 minutes	2-4 minutes
Cool-down	10-15 minutes	10-15 minutes	10-15 minutes

WEDNESDAY

Rest

THURSDAY

Same as Monday

FRIDAY

Same as Tuesday

SATURDAY

Rest

SUNDAY

Rest

Competitive Period April 15–September (competition lengths vary): Perform strength training at 75 percent of your one-repetition maximum. Perform aerobic training at 75 percent of your HRR. Perform anaerobic training at 90 percent of your HRR.

MONDAY

Rest

TUESDAY

Ski only

WEDNESDAY

	Week 1-2	*Week 3-4*	*Week 5-6*
Warm-up	10-15 minutes	10-15 minutes	10-15 minutes
Sit-ups	3 × max	3 × max	3 × max
Squats or leg press	2 × 10-15	2 × 10-15	2 × 10-15
Bench press	1 × 10-15	1 × 10-15	1 × 10-15
Military press	1 × 10-15	1 × 10-15	1 × 10-15
Arm curls	1 × 10-15	1 × 10-15	1 × 10-15
Triceps extensions	1 × 10-15	1 × 10-15	1 × 10-15
Back extensions	1 × 10-15	1 × 10-15	1 × 10-15
Interval training	5-10 intervals	5-10 intervals	5-10 intervals
Cool-down	10-15 intervals	10-15 intervals	10-15 intervals

THURSDAY

Ski only

FRIDAY

Rest

SATURDAY

Compete

SUNDAY

Compete

Active Rest Period November 1–December 31: After one to four weeks of complete rest, perform strength-training exercises at 60 percent of your one-repetition maximum. Perform aerobic exercises at 70 percent of your HRR.

MONDAY

	Week 1-2	Week 3-4	Week 5-6
Warm-up	10-15 minutes	10-15 minutes	10-15 minutes
Sit-ups	3 × max	3 × max	3 × max
Squats or leg press	3-5 × 15-20	3-5 × 15-20	1 × max
Leg curls	2 × 15-20	2 × 15-20	1 × max
Leg extensions	2 × 15-20	2 × 15-20	2 × 15-20
Bench press	2 × 15-20	2 × 15-20	2 × 15-20
Military press	2 × 15-20	2 × 15-20	2 × 15-20
Lat pull down	2 × 15-20	2 × 15-20	2 × 15-20
Arm curls	2 × 15-20	2 × 15-20	2 × 15-20
Triceps extensions	2 × 15-20	2 × 15-20	2 × 15-20
Back extensions	2 × 15-20	2 × 15-20	2 × 15-20
Leg extensions	2 × 15-20	2 × 15-20	2 × 15-20
Bench press	2 × 15-20	2 × 15-20	2 × 15-20
Military press	2 × 15-20	2 × 15-20	2 × 15-20
Lat pull down	2 × 15-20	2 × 15-20	2 × 15-20
Arm curls	2 × 15-20	2 × 15-20	2 × 15-20
Triceps extensions	2 × 15-20	2 × 15-20	2 × 15-20
Back extensions	2 × 15-20	2 × 15-20	2 × 15-20
Cool-down	15-20 minutes	15-20 minutes	15-20 minutes

TUESDAY

	Week 1-2	Week 3-4	Week 5-6
Warm-up	10 minutes	10 minutes	10 minutes
Aerobic training	25 minutes	30 minutes	40 minutes
Cool-down	10 minutes	10 minutes	10 minutes

WEDNESDAY

Rest

THURSDAY

Same as Monday

FRIDAY

Same as Tuesday

SATURDAY

Rest

SUNDAY

Rest

Here are eight ways to avoid injury, staleness, and overtraining:

1. If your training program begins to leave you tired and cranky, add another day of rest to your weekly schedule.
2. Take one week per month for recovery; during this week ski and work out at 30 to 40 percent of your normal weekly volume.
3. Do not try to build up your training at a time when stress at home, work, or school is also on the upswing.
4. Carefully monitor your training volume. The simplest way to increase your training load is to add more volume, but it's also the surest route to overtraining.
5. To improve your performance, concentrate on short technique sets instead of volume.
6. When you wake up in the morning, check your mood and muscle soreness. If increased soreness coincides with a darkened mood, take the day off and train very lightly for the next couple of days.
7. When you take a rest day, really rest. Do not replace the stress of training with the stress of trying to accomplish a million other things. Relax, read, nap, meditate, listen to music, and talk with friends. Make sure you end the day feeling calm and rested.
8. Do not make the skier's biggest mistake: forcing yourself to train harder because you've had a bad set or tournament. If you feel fatigued during ski sets and your scores are down, do not ski anymore. Instead, rest for several days, and return with a fresh body and winning attitude.

How do you know if you're a victim of overtraining? Here are some things to check:

1. Waking heart rate. If your waking pulse on any day is more than eight beats per minute above its average for the preceding week, you are falling into overtraining. Take your pulse before you get out of bed for the most accurate measure.
2. Waking body weight. If your body weight drops by more than three pounds on any day from a previously stable body weight, you are falling into overtraining.
3. Insomnia. If you do not train at night yet start to suffer from restlessness, inability to fall asleep, or too-early awakening, you are falling into overtraining.

If you are overtraining, what should you do? Here are five things that should provide the cure:

1. Stop training entirely for one week. Stretch for 30 minutes a day as your only activity.

2. Reduce protein intake to 15 percent of total calories
3. Increase carbohydrate intake to 70 percent of total calories. Use predominately complex carbs.
4. Increase antioxidants to 200 percent of usual intake. (Take two Protegra tablets daily.)
5. Increase sleep to nine hours solid per night.

Overtraining can destroy a season. Knowing how to push your limits and not fall into overtraining will give you a competitive advantage in strength and confidence. Pay attention to your training and listen to your body. Follow the above guidelines and you will see terrific results. For an even greater impact, follow a nutrition plan designed for skiing like the one given below.

WATER SKIING NUTRITION

Water skiing is vastly different from endurance sports such as running or cycling; thus the nutritional requirements for skiers are considerably different. Water skiing requires you to expend bursts of discontinuous explosive energy, with intermittent periods of rest or reduced physical demand. In slalom you drop at the end of the course after a completed pass; in jump you have time between jumps when riding down the lake; in tricking you have setup time between passes or the intentional fall to catch your breath. Skiing requires endurance—you spend long days in the boat or on the lake in the energy-draining sun—but it's not the same type of endurance one needs for running a marathon or cross-country skiing over long distances. Robert Haas, MD, author of *Eat to Win*, recommends a balanced diet with the right mixture of protein, fat, and carbohydrate. Such a diet will replenish torn-down muscles and train muscles to use blood sugar and fat efficiently to provide explosive power.

Three food categories—carbohydrates, proteins, and fats—supply the fuel for peak performance. Eat these foods in the suggested quantities to meet the nutritional requirements of water skiing.

Carbohydrates (50 to 75 percent of total caloric intake)

Cereals
Fresh fruit
Dried fruit
Fruit juice
Potatoes

Brown rice
Pasta
Vegetables (raw or steamed)
Whole-grain breads or pancakes

Proteins (15 to 35 percent of total caloric intake)

Skim milk
Low-fat cheese
Grated Parmesan or Romano cheese
Low-fat cottage cheese
Low-fat yogurt
Meat: poultry, fish, shellfish, lean beef, duck, pork, lamb, venison
Legumes: beans, peas, lentils, nuts, seeds

Fats (5 to 20 percent of total caloric intake)

Olive oil
Vegetable oil, corn oil, safflower oil
Margarine
Mayonnaise
Avoid peanut oil, butter, and lard

Other food items

These will help improve the taste of foods and are OK in limited quantities.

Butter buds
Oil-free salad dressings
Vinegar
Condiments (mustard, ketchup, steak sauce, barbecue sauce)
Lemon or lime juice
Bacon bits or soy bits
Sugar and salt-free spices

Drinks

Water is the preferred beverage. Other drinks that are OK in limited quantities include the following:

Coffee
Vegetable juices
Hot chocolate (lite versions)
Diet soda (without caffeine)

Nutritional Supplements

Nutritional supplements have evolved in the last few years. Current research has demonstrated that a total nutrient taken two to four times per day is better than trying to piece together a mix of vitamins and other supplements. They are also more convenient since they eliminate measuring, counting, and weighing of foods. Products such as Met-Rx, and copycat versions, offer a scientifically engineered balance of vitamins, minerals, carbohydrates, protein, and trace elements that your body needs to maximize your potential. These products are designed for nutrient partitioning and come in either bar or powder form. Nutrient partitioning pushes the essential nutrients toward lean muscle tissue instead of fat. This change in the metabolic environment causes energy to be stored selectively in the muscle tissue rather than as fat. Because of this phenomenon, and the sheer volume of the shakes (which reduces your total caloric intake), many skiers lose weight and or gain lean muscle mass when taking these supplements.

Precompetition Meal

Pro skiers are as superstitious as other athletes. Skiers are not above believing that eating a particular meal is the lucky charm that spells the difference between a good performance and a flop. I ate a huge prime rib in Hartford, Connecticut, the night before I made my first Pro Tour final. The next year I realized I had eaten a steak the night before finishing second at Marine World, my highest tour finish at the time. From that tournament on, I would try to eat a steak before every tournament. Is there a magic meal that might be better than my steak?

Scientists have thoroughly researched both the timing and content of the precompetition meal. Their findings have not revealed any one menu that is right for everyone. But they all agree that a nutritionally sound precompetition meal will not compensate for poor dietary habits the weeks leading up to the competition. Research has shown that the food and beverages you consume the weeks before an event affect performance. Nutritionists suggest, however, that you should not underestimate the psychological benefits of the precompetition meal. Performance depends on feeling at your peak physically, mentally, and emotionally. The routine and camaraderie of dining with family or friends on a diet of well-liked foods may give you the edge over the competition. Nutritionists offer this tip: Eat familiar foods and drink plenty of water.

When planning your precompetition meal, first select foods you like and tolerate well. Eat something you are accustomed to eating to prevent gastrointestinal distress such as diarrhea. Don't go off to a tournament and try the local fruit or meal before you compete. Wait until after the competition. Your diet should be rich in carbohydrates such as bread and pasta, but low in fat. Drink as much water or juice as comfortably possible to ensure you are properly hydrated. Dehydration sabotages the performances of many athletes before they even start their event, so make sure you take plenty of fluids the day of your competition and the days leading up to it. If your urine is clear and you are going to the bathroom every two to four hours, you are well hydrated. If you get hungry just before your event or throughout the day, you should eat carbo-rich snacks and keep pumping in the fluids.

You should have your last meal no less than two hours before your event. This time frame allows you to empty your stomach before the time of competition, yet you won't feel weak or hungry. This is another matter you must play with to determine what works best for you. The key is to feel strong, fresh, and ready to perform your best. Once you determine a pattern for your digestion and how you feel after a meal, you know the recipe for your perfect precompetition meal. I'm sticking with my steak the night before, but you need to find out what works for you.

CHAPTER 4

BASIC SKIING SKILLS

Good water skiing shows the signature characteristics of flow of movement, confidence, power, sensitivity, and precision. No matter what your ability, you will need to develop these qualities to enhance your skills. One of the primary goals of this book is to establish a learning system for these characteristics that is progressive and based on solid technical and biomechanical foundations. By using this system you will be able to eliminate the senseless frustration caused by training or learning a new trick or slalom pass based on a whim or contrived method you heard from another skier. Our step-by-step learning system is rooted in the four fundamental motor skills used in water skiing: balance, edge control, pressure control, and rotation.

SKILLS OF SKIING

No one of these four skills is more important than the others. You should strive for a balanced blend, with the four skills working together to improve your skiing. Therefore, at times you will need to stress certain skills. Most skiers, when first learning to ski, have difficulty with rotary or turning movements. Once they learn how to turn, it becomes apparent that they must develop edge control and pressure control so they can get across the wakes. To do so, they must improve balance so they can maintain body position. You will naturally be better at some skills than others. Each skier develops a different set of abilities and movement skills from his or her sport and life experiences. The principles and fundamentals from other sports oftentimes cross over. The body position of a jumper is very similar to that of a snow skier. In both, the skier sets a hard edge to maintain direction or angle. The arched back, leg extension, and rhythm of rowing are similar to a slalom. The rotational axis of an ice skater is nearly identical to that of a tricker.

Although some of you will be familiar with the skills and drills in this book, few are truly proficient in performing them. I encourage you to make your first step toward achieving your water skiing goals a backward one. Go through the skills progression we have laid out. The awareness you develop by reviewing the fundamental drills and skills will surprise you. This one step back is time well spent. You will develop a better understanding of how and why to use each skill and learn more quickly when you attempt more advanced maneuvers. We begin by examining each skill used in water skiing and how it fits into basic water skiing body position.

Balance

Balance is the skill required to keep the body in equilibrium when acted upon by external forces. Brent Larsen, coach and father of the world-record-setting trickers Britt and Tawn, defines water skiing as balance in motion. Balance is that important in skiing. The forces that affect balance may be the result of deliberate actions on the skier's part (turning or changing edges), or they may be the result of reaction to disturbances (change in boat speed or water conditions). The balancing movements may involve relatively gross body adjustments or almost imperceptible adjustments, depending on the circumstances. Bouncing on a trampoline is a great tool for learning balance and getting a feel for controlling your body movement in space. The secret to improved balance is body position. Work on these points to improve your balance on your skis:

- Keep your legs soft and reactive, neither locked out nor rigid, for all types of skiing.
- Maintain an erect upper body, but keep your knees and ankles flexed for better muscular and skeletal efficiency.
- Involve the entire foot (use neither a forward nor backward weight shift) in balancing actions to develop the ability to work the entire ski.
- Hold your upper body still and calm as it moves in a dynamic relationship with the skis.
- Focus your eyes on the horizon.

Figure 4.1   Balance is required to keep the body in equilibrium when acted upon by external forces.

Edge Control

Edge control is the skill that affects the way the edges of the skis contact the water's surface. The concept of controlling the edging movements is important because the interaction between the ski edges and the water surface forces the skis to turn or rotate. Skiers use two methods for edge control: inclination and angulation. Most slalom skiers use inclination, as shown in figure 4.2. This means a taller stance than tricking or jumping with skeletal alignment. This is a powerful position to set an edge and maintain angle. Most trickers and jumpers use angulation, as shown in figure 4.3, which means the skier creates angles between body segments. The upper body remains vertical, while the skier uses hips, knees, and ankles to create angles and set the edge. For efficient edge control movements concentrate on these points:

Figure 4.2   Inclination, used by most slalom skiers, uses skeletal alignment to set an edge and maintain angle.

Figure 4.3   Angulation, used by trickers and jumpers, uses the hips, knees, and ankles to create angles and set an edge while the upper body remains vertical.

- Keep hips and shoulders in alignment with the skis during the edge change.
- Make adjustments in edge control with the hips, knees, and ankles.
- Guide the ski progressively onto edge-preturn-edge and use pressure adjustments to assist in achieving the desired turn shape and angle across course.

Pressure Control

Skiers use pressure control skills to regulate and adjust the pressure of the skis on the water as they move through it. Pressure control works very closely with edge control to maintain angle and direction across course as the boat pulls you downcourse. For precise pressure control, work on the following:

- Use smooth and progressive pressure shift to the outside ski or edge as the turn develops.
- Use a more aggressive weight transfer as you advance to upper-level skiing.
- Use flexion-extension of the knees and ankles to complement other actions in control of turn shape.
- As angle increases, you need greater pressure control.

Figure 4.4   Pressure control works closely with edge control to maintain angle and direction.

Rotation

Rotation skills involve the rotation, or the tendency toward rotation, of either the body as a whole or one part of the body relative to another. As with balance, rotation may be subtle or quite strong, and active or reactive, depending on the situation and the skier's wishes. For efficiency and stability, use the lower body to generate rotation. To enhance rotation, stress the following:

- Link slalom and jump turns with a continuous flow of the body's center of mass, the hips, across course.
- In slalom, move the hips toward the next turn during turn initiation to facilitate edge change and enhance the change of direction.
- For tricking, use the hips to drive the turn; the shoulders and head follow.
- The tricker should maintain the axis through the head, shoulders, hips, and ankles for efficient rotation.
- Begin rotation slowly and finish strongly.

Figure 4.5 Rotation skills are obvious in tricks like this, but they are also needed for slalom and jump turns.

LEARNING STYLES

Technically speaking, water skiing is a highly sophisticated and complex outcome-based movement task that requires the skier to perceive, interpret, and perform a variety of movement combinations with accuracy, finesse, timing, and power.

A skillful performance in water skiing is the result of developing the awareness and perception required to interpret environmental factors such as wind and water conditions, to assess the performance of equipment, and to determine the skill movement best suited for the situation.

This technical explanation makes it seem that skiing should be impossible. Of course, it isn't. It is a learned skill that you must practice and learn properly if your goal is to learn a new slalom pass, master a flip, bust a 100-foot jump, or throw a huge air ralley. Determining how you naturally prefer to learn will assist you in efficiently learning these new skills. To do this, we need to examine learning styles.

In learning a new motor skill you will go through a four-stage process along the learning curve:

1. Unconscious incompetence. You are unaware of what you need to do or how to perform the skill.
2. Conscious incompetence. You understand the theory of what to do but lack the physical ability to perform the skill.
3. Conscious competence. You are able to perform the skill only when making an effort to think about what to do.
4. Unconscious competence. The skill becomes natural and you automatically perform the skill without thinking about it.

To move along the learning curve efficiently and eliminate unnecessary frustration, slumps, or plateaus, we must develop an understanding of how we learn best, what our preferred learning style is. In the *AWSA Level III Coaches Manual,* Rick Jensen, PhD states, "To optimize our learning it is important to understand how we best learn." Let's discuss the process of how a skier learns new skills.

We receive instructions through the senses (sight, sound, touch), process them, and store them in the brain. When we want to draw on this information during training, we retrieve the instructions stored in the brain and use them to guide behavior.

Knowing this, we can determine learning styles or the primary ways in which people think, respond, and make sense of their experiences. The learning styles used in skiing are visual (learned by watching), auditory (learned by listening), and kinesthetic (learned by feel). We use all three learning styles, but have a preferred style at which we are most efficient. To benefit from your learning style, take the test on pages 66 and 67 and incorporate the training strategies into your training program.

DETERMINING YOUR LEARNING STYLE

Learning Styles Questionnaire

Please rank order (from most like you to least like you) each statement within each question using the scale below. Use the scoresheet at the end of the questionnaire to record your scores. (Within each question, you should have one item ranked as a 1, one ranked as a 2, and one ranked as a 3.)

1-most like me	2-somewhat like me	3-least like me

1. **While receiving water ski instruction, I prefer to**
   a. view myself on video and observe the changes that I need to make
   b. be told exactly what to do and how it will improve my performance
   c. get on the water and execute practice drills to develop a feel for the correct technique

2. **When I recall my first water ski lesson, the thing that I remember best is**
   a. something I heard
   b. something I felt
   c. something I saw

3. **I learn new skills best by**
   a. skiing and practicing as much as possible
   b. watching demonstrations of correct technique and top performances
   c. discussing technique and performance strategies with knowledgeable skiers

LEARNING STRATEGIES

Once you have determined your preferred learning style or styles, you can begin to select the training strategies that will be most effective for you. You should begin applying strategies that are consistent with your primary learning style; this will enhance your ability to absorb information and more rapidly make technical adjustments. As your training on a specific event or technique progresses, you should gradually expand your training strategies to include the full range of learning

4. **When ski instruction tips are given on television, I attend most to**
   a. positions demonstrated during slow-motion replay
   b. expert commentary given by top skiers or coaches
   c. drills provided that I can execute during my practice sessions

5. **Of the following water ski materials, I would prefer to have**
   a. an audiotape of interviews of top skiers discussing their views of the proper techniques
   b. a training aid developed by top skiers that assists me in developing the feeling of the proper technique
   c. a videotape (with no verbal instruction) demonstrating top skiers' performances from a variety of camera angles

SCORING

Visual score:
Add your scores to questions 1a + 2c + 3b + 4a + 5c = _____

Auditory score:
Add your scores to questions 1b + 2a + 3c + 4b + 5a = _____

Kinesthetic score:
Add your scores to questions 1c + 2b + 3a + 4c + 5b = _____

The scores for each of the three learning styles will fall between 5 and 15 with the sum of all three styles totaling 30. Lower scores indicate a greater preference for that particular learning style. A large difference among the scores suggests a strong preference for receiving instruction in the style with the lowest score. If, however, you find that your scores are relatively close to one another, then you can benefit from using a variety of training strategies that incorporate several of the learning preferences.

Courtesy of the American Water Ski Association.

styles—visual, auditory, and kinesthetic—thus creating a greater training experience.

Visual Training Strategies

1. Ask your coach or a more advanced skier to demonstrate the appropriate technique.
2. Study pictures, illustrations, figures, and so forth.
3. Watch videotape.
4. Find and use role models with similar skiing styles for demonstrations.

5. Use mirrors to check body position and posture.
6. Place objects on the water as visual targets.
7. Seek advanced training in visualization and imagery.
8. Learn to eliminate negative images of poor performances or poor technique.
9. Obtain detailed material in a visual manner (overheads, films, tournament statistics, etc.).

Auditory Training Strategies

1. Seek opportunities for discussions with other knowledgeable skiers.
2. Put techniques, exercises, routines, and so forth to music or sounds.
3. Obtain written information about water skiing, mental training, and so forth.
4. Use audiotapes, headphones, and so forth.
5. Have discussions about rules, strategies, technical changes, and so forth.
6. Discuss logic and purpose for learning a particular technique.
7. Follow up training periods and competition with discussions.
8. Seek specific and constant verbal feedback regarding progress.
9. Obtain advanced training for developing positive self-talk procedures and eliminating negative self-talk or distracting thoughts.

Kinesthetic Training Strategies

1. Make sure that you practice correctly so that you learn the feeling of the correct techniques and skills.
2. Allow plenty of time for supervised practice to ensure that you learn the correct positions.
3. When receiving feedback from others, hold yourself in position as you try to obtain correct technique.
4. Identify and discuss feelings that accompany particular movements.
5. Learn how to store in your mind the feelings associated with correct performance of new techniques.
6. Use and control emotions during competition.
7. Obtain advanced training for managing anxiety and distracting emotions.
8. Learn relaxation, breathing, and stretching exercises.
9. Use tangible devices, cues, and training aids during training periods.

Now you are ready. You have the right mindset for learning, you know the course you are taking, you have the right equipment, you know how to be safe, you are strong and in great physical shape, you know the skills to be mastered, and you have some strategies to speed up the process. Let's take it to the water and begin working on your slalom, tricking, jumping, and boarding.

CHAPTER 5

SLALOM SKIING

Why is slalom the most popular type of skiing? You can compare slalom to another wildly popular sport, IndyCar racing. In both you have the incredible G-force of acceleration followed by a dramatic near stop as you slow for a sharp hairpin turn and then blast off again toward the next turn. While only a few ever get to ride in an IndyCar, anyone can feel the exhilaration on a slalom ski. Whoa! Before we get caught up in the thrills of slalom, let's first learn the basics.

SLALOM FUNDAMENTALS

The objective of this section is to teach the person who is comfortable on two skis to set themselves free from the bulky confines of combos. You will learn the fundamentals of getting up on a slalom ski, correct slalom body position, and the stages of learning to run the slalom course.

Skill 1: Skier Salute

When someone tries to teach you how to rise out of the water on one ski, it looks and sounds extremely difficult. The fact is, however, that it is a simple progression that you can learn quickly and easily. The first step is becoming comfortable doing the "skier salute." This is simply lifting one ski out of the water as you ski down the lake. Try it on land first. As with most new skills in water skiing, it is a great idea to try it on land first. Land practice gives you a feel of what you are doing and eliminates needless falls and frustrations.

Keep your head and eyes focused on the horizon. Bend your knees and ankles. Now, keeping your arms straight, slowly shift all your weight over

Figure 5.1   The skier salute.

either leg and slowly lift the opposite leg. Keep your toes pointed up so you don't stick a tip. Try this with both legs to determine which foot should be in front and which ski you will soon be dropping. An on-land method to select which foot goes in front is to stand up straight and have someone push you from behind. Whichever leg you catch yourself on should be the foot that goes in the front binding. The key is comfort. There is no right or wrong; simply use whichever foot feels better to you.

Skill 2: Dropping a Ski

Begin this lesson on land also. Go through the same process you did with the skier salute. Keep your head up, arms straight, and knees and ankles bent. Shift all your weight to one ski and very smoothly and slowly lift your heel out of the opposite binding. Once you're on the water, repeat the same movements. You can allow the free foot to drag in the water to help with balance and control. Once you have control, place your foot on the back of the ski and move it into the rear toe loop behind the other foot. You should have equal weight on both feet with your back straight, knees bent, and head up. Once you are slalom skiing, maintain correct body position as shown in the figure 5.2. It's that easy! But here are a few tips if things are not going so smoothly:

- If your skis are wobbly or you keep losing your balance, try moving more slowly and keeping your weight evenly distributed over the ski.

Figure 5.2   Dropping a ski.

- If you are falling to the side of the dropped ski, you need to put more weight on the ski leg before attempting to drop the ski.
- If trouble persists, try a wider, longer ski such as a jumper or a big man's slalom.

- Keep extra drop skis in the boat and always try to drop your skis in a familiar area where you can find them.
- If all else fails, have a qualified instructor or skier aid you by holding your vest to help you balance as you drop the ski.

Skill 3: Deep-Water Start

Some people believe the deep-water start is difficult to learn. Whenever I hear this I chuckle and say, "You had the wrong teacher." When taught correctly, the deep-water start is as easy as standing up from a chair.

The trick to learning a deep-water start quickly is adjusting to the feel of having the boat pull you out of the water. A skillful driver can simulate this sensation. After you drop a ski and are comfortable riding on one ski and maybe even crossing the wakes, position yourself be-

Figure 5.3   The deep-water start.

hind the boat in perfect body position. Now have the driver gradually slow the boat to 10 to 15 mph and then power back up as if he or she were pulling a deep-water start. Continue to do this, slowing down more and more until you are nearly all the way in the water before being pulled back out. This drill is an excellent simulation that teaches you which muscles are being pulled and how much resistance you need to apply to keep from being pulled forward.

Now it's time to learn how to rise from the water by yourself. The key is patience! Nearly all falls getting up on a slalom are caused by rushing the start and trying to stand up too quickly. Hurried movements force the ski tip down and the skier over the front. Stay calm and relaxed and let the boat pull you over the ski and out of the water. The process is like this: Bend the ski leg (the one with the ski) completely, with the knee touching the chest. Place the rope on the inside of the ski, and extend the free leg out behind you as a stabilizer or place it in the rear binding. Keep arms straight or slightly bent and place body weight over the middle of the ski. As always, focus head and eyes up. Now, say "Hit it!" and you are off.

The slalom deep-water start is quite different from the two-ski deep-water start. You must remember that since you are on one ski it will take longer to reach a plane on the water's surface. So take your time— wait until the ski is moving fast enough to support your weight before you rise out of the water.

TROUBLESHOOTING THE DEEP-WATER START

FALL: Forward.
Error: Stood up too quickly, weight too far forward.
Solution: Take your time. Stand up slowly, moving your shoulders back as the ski planes.

FALL: Side.
Error: Free leg not in correct position.
Solution: Keep free leg straight and back with the knee in.

FALL: Backward.
Error: Pulled with your arms, rope on wrong side.
Solution: Keep arms straight, *always*! Rope should be on free-leg side.

FALL: Plowing.
Error: Knee too far from chest, ski too vertical.
Solution: Keep knee into chest and allow the ski to be parallel to the water's surface.

If you are still having problems, try a few of these ski school secrets to eliminate falls and frustration encountered in learning to slalom:

- Start on a boom as shown in figure 5.4. This method is as easy as it gets. Once you get up holding onto the boom, put on a handle extension and try it. Once you have that down, go behind the boat.
- Shorten the rope so the pull is more direct and quick. This will eliminate the feeling of slack line.
- Have the instructor put the rope over his or her shoulder so the pull is from a higher point, pulling you up, rather than across, the water.
- Have an instructor hold your vest to help you balance as you come out of the water. This is great for kids, but hard to do for larger people.
- Try putting your back foot in the rear binding. Sometimes this one change is enough to get you up. The key in starting this way is to keep your knees together and into your chest.

Now you are a slalom skier. Go out there and cut it up, cross the wakes, and have a ball. What? You say you are scared of the wakes and don't feel comfortable crossing them? Don't worry; that's our next lesson.

Figure 5.4 If you're having problems with the deep-water start, try starting on a boom.

Skill 4: Body Position

Without a doubt, the most important part of slalom skiing is learning to lean and hold angle through the wakes. When you are first learning, the wakes feel like mountains, and you are certain that they are going to toss you off your ski. Well, you are right—the wakes will launch you off your ski if you don't have proper body position and lean. Learning how to lean and cross the wakes effortlessly is a simple three-step process.

Step 1.   Begin on land or in the boat. Tie a handle to a door, a post, or the boat pylon and imitate figure 5.5. Notice a few things. The head and eyes are parallel to the water, the arms are straight, the hips are close to the handle, and there is considerable flexion of the knees and ankles. Hold this position for a minute or so and feel where the pull and strain are. It should be in your legs, and to a lesser extent, in your upper back. Now do the same thing pointing the other direction and get comfortable leaning that way. You need to practice this drill constantly and work to improve your body position. The sooner you feel strong and confident in this position, the easier slalom will be.

Figure 5.5   Practicing this lean drill on land will help you improve your on-water body position.

Step 2. The next step in learning to cross the wakes in a leaning position is done behind the boat. Shorten the rope to 28 off (the yellow loop). This will take away the slack-rope feeling and keep the rope tight during the drill. Have the driver run the boat at 24 to 28 mph for an adult and slower for children. Position yourself at the base of the wake. While standing there, shift into correct body position. Get your head up, let your arms out straight, bring your hips to the handle, and bend your knees and ankles. Find a point on the shore on your side of the wake and start leaning to it. Hold that position. Continue to hold it until you are as far up on the side of the boat as you can get. It's that simple! Maintain the position down the full length of the lake. After you turn around, go to the other side of the wake and do the same thing. You will notice it is easier on one side than the other. That is natural and very common. Everyone has a good side and an off side that is determined by which foot they put forward in their ski. The secret is to get comfortable and confident on both sides. Granted, it may take a little longer to get a strong, leveraged body position on your off side, but it will happen with practice.

Step 3. The final part of this drill is actually crossing the wakes. Have no fear—you now have all the skills you need, and most important, the

Figure 5.6   After practicing correct position on land, take it to the water: head up, hips up to the handle, knees and ankles bent.

correct body position to slice right through those bumps of water behind the boat. Start off at the base of the wake, as you did in step 2. Get into your newly developed perfect body position and pull 25 to 35 feet outside the wake. Go into a glide with your ski flat on the water's surface. As you begin to slow down and are pulled back toward the wakes, make a slow turn and lean through the wakes the same way you did on the side of the boat. Remember to keep your head up and look across to a point on the shore. Keep leaning through the wakes until you are all the way up on the side of the boat as in step 2. Come out of your lean and off your edge. Again, make a slow turn and head back the other way. Keep practicing. This drill takes time to perfect, but once you get it down, learning to run the course is a breeze. Here are a few quick tips that may make it easier.

1. Keep your arms straight! This is the most common error. Think about leaning against the rope with your arms relaxed.
2. To prevent breaking at the waist, flex your front knee more or drive your hips up to the handle more.
3. Keep your ski on edge to cure bouncing over the wakes. Being pulled to a flat ski is the cause of this. Think about leaning more and harder. Try to show the bottom of your ski to the observer by tilting the ski on its side through the wakes.

Figure 5.7   If you've learned how to hold correct body position outside the wakes, cutting the wakes is no problem.

4. Keep your upper body calm and still. The only body parts that should move as you go through the wakes are the knees. The idea is to lock out the upper body and shift the stress and strain of the boat's pull to your strongest muscles, your legs. You can think of it as a tug-of-war in which you push with the legs rather than pull with the arms.

SKIING THE SLALOM COURSE

You have now mastered the fundamental skills needed to begin learning how to run the slalom course. You can get up on one ski, arrange yourself in proper body position, and lean across the wakes while maintaining correct body position. This is when the real fun begins—slalom course skiing.

As we said, skiing the slalom course is very similar to IndyCar racing—the rocket-like acceleration, the gripping turns, the adrenaline rush of controlled speed. These are the physical addictions of slalom, but the slalom course provides a bonus—the mental enchantment of, say, golf. In golf, the course always wins; the same is true for slalom. Like golf, slalom constantly challenges you to improve. You can never be too good. Skiers become mesmerized by the slalom course, constantly looking for a new and better way to run that next pass or get to that next buoy. The lure of slalom course skiing begins here, by learning how to run the minicourse, then shadowing or running the narrow course, and finally running the full slalom course.

Skill 1: Skiing the Minicourse

The minicourse is simply half of the full slalom course. The boat is driven down the right side of the course between the boat guide buoys on the left, and the skier turn buoys on the right. The driver should start at 20 to 26 mph for adults and hold the speed constant. You need to get in correct body position and pull out to the right side of the boat about 25 feet. As the #1 buoy approaches, you will make a turn around the buoy, finishing the turn so you are skiing across course as you pass the downcourse side of the buoy, as shown in figure 5.8. Here is the critical area. You must maintain correct body position and lean as hard as possible through both wakes without breaking your body position. Hold your direction across the course and look 20 feet before the next buoy, the left boat guide buoy. Once across the second wake, immediately change edge and let the ski make a smooth turn around the #2 buoy and back across the course. Repeat the same process across the wakes—keep your head up, arms straight, knees flexed, and lean across the wakes looking to a point in front of the #3 buoy. Make another smooth turn and head for #4. Again, lean through the wakes, turn, and lean again to #5 and then #6. You did it! You have taken your first steps to becoming a slalom god.

Keep running the minicourse until you can make it at about 26 mph. Remember to focus on leaning through the wakes and maintaining correct body position. The minicourse teaches you the rhythm of slalom that is vital for running the big course. An important point is that the slalom course, and even the minicourse, is about making six turns and six pulls. Rarely does anyone, even the world's best, make six perfect turns and pulls. You need to be a fighter. Never give up on a pass until you miss a buoy or fall. So when you have a bobble or break out of proper position, do not quit! Make a strong lean or a hard turn and get back into the pass. You will be amazed at the number of buoys you will run when you just keep fighting.

Skill 2: Skiing the Shadow Course or Narrow Course

The next phase of learning to run the slalom course is to shadow the big course or run the narrow course. The narrow course is the same as the regular course but the buoys are 10 feet narrower, as shown in the diagram. If you don't have a narrow course, just drop some buoys in or imagine the buoys are in place.

Have the driver go through the boat guide buoys at 24 to 28 mph. This may feel slow, but if you are leaning hard enough and long enough, you will generate plenty of speed to carry you through the turns. Start with the rope at either long line (75 feet) or 15 off (the first cut loop, red). I recommend pulling all the way outside the #1 full-course buoy, even though you will be running or shadowing the narrow course. Get yourself at least 3 feet wide of the first buoy and start the turn 10 feet before the buoy, as you did on the minicourse, so you will finish the turn on the backside of the buoy. From there, it is five more turns, six leans, and out the exit gates.

As with the minicourse, the turns need to be smooth and slow, with strong, powerful leans through the wakes. The emphasis is on holding your direction across the wakes. Resist the pull from the boat, especially at the second wake. By driving your shoulder away from the boat, down and back, as you cross the wakes, you will be able to hold the angle and lean longer. Since you are skiing from a wider position, you will have a tendency to generate your angle too soon, and the boat may pull you up at the wakes. The solution is to have a progressive lean with your greatest resistance through the wakes as shown in figure 5.10. When you get across the wakes and are waiting for the next

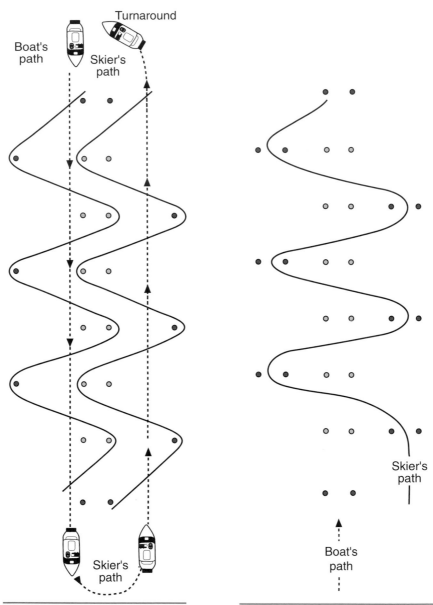

Figure 5.8   The minicourse.

Figure 5.9   The narrow course.

buoy, don't get lazy and stand up; stay down in your ski with your knees and ankles flexed. Remember to start your turns well before the oncoming buoy. I like to simplify slalom to a turn and a lean. Don't try to think of a preturn—just lean through both wakes, change direction in your turn, and lean the other way.

Constantly work on body position: hips forward, shoulders back, knees flexed, arms straight. Body position is everything. Once you get

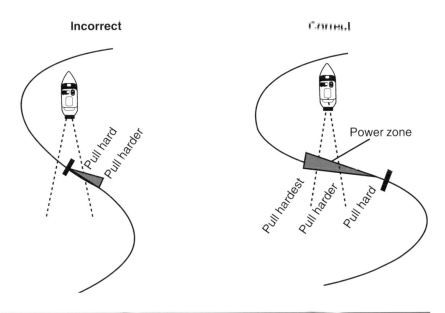

Incorrect   **Correct**

Power zone

Pull hard
Pull harder

Pull hardest
Pull harder
Pull hard

Figure 5.10 With a progressive lean you'll have your greatest resistance through the wakes.

comfortable with that strong, leveraged position, everything slows down, and there is not as much stress on your body because you are using the larger muscles.

Skill 3: Skiing the Full Slalom Course

You're ready! You have built a talent and skill foundation that stresses the fundamentals. You are now ready to conquer the full slalom course shown in figure 5.11. Running the full course is no different from running the minicourse or the shadow course, except that the intensity level changes. The fundamentals are the same:

1. Body position is critical. Keep your arms straight, knees and ankles flexed, hips up to the handle, and head and eyes parallel with the horizon.
2. Hold your angle and direction through both wakes and especially at the second wake.
3. Establish a rhythm in your turn and lean.
4. Never give up on a pass!

Now we are going to learn how to run the course backward. I don't mean facing backward; I mean learning how to ski around #6, after shadowing #5, #4, #3, and #2. Figure 5.12 illustrates this concept for every step. Figure 5.12a shows the path of a skier starting wide of the

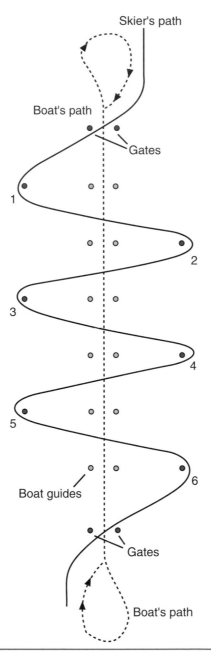

Figure 5.11   The full slalom course.

#1 buoy, then shadowing the remaining buoys. Figure 5.12b shows the first part of the progression. Start wide of the #1 buoy as usual and run the narrow course, but when you lean from #5 to #6 keep leaning until you get outside #6. Once you can do this, start out at #1, shadow #2, #3, and #4, and ski around #5 and #6. Keep backing up and practicing until you get around all six buoys. Before you know it you will run a complete pass.

You may have noticed that I have not mentioned anything about how to turn and how to go through the gates. Don't worry; we'll cover how to ski the gates in the next lesson. Now let's talk about the turn.

I have not said much about the turn for three reasons. First, most people do it naturally. Second, most skiers focus on the turn when the real emphasis needs to be on creating angle and holding it through the wakes with correct body position. Last, slalom gets very complicated when you break down every movement. I prefer to keep it simple by concentrating on body position through the wakes and thinking of the turn as a simple change of direction. You need to think about only three things in the turn: (1) execute the edge change quickly and smoothly, (2) concentrate on staying down in your ski with your knees and ankles flexed to aid in the deceleration of the ski, and (3) make your reach to the side and slightly up to aid in keeping your head up in the turn. From there, you simply get the handle back quickly to your hips and get into your lean. I believe in the benefits of two-handed turns. You should begin using one-handed turns only after you can run the course with two hands. But do whatever it takes to make six buoys when you are first learning. When you have learned the rhythm of making six turns and leans in the confines of the slalom course, you are ready to conquer the gates and begin working on developing consistency, strength, and timing in your skiing.

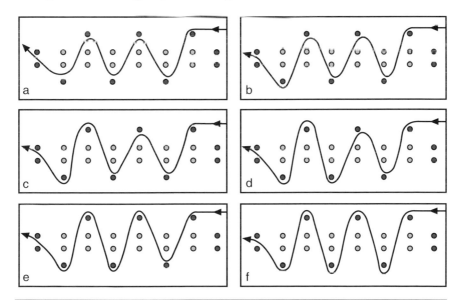

Figure 5.12   Run the course backward, progressively adding buoys, until you have skied around all six buoys.

Skill 4: Skiing the Gates

Once you have strong, leveraged body position, the most difficult and important part of the slalom course is the gates. Any Pro Tour skier will tell you that the gates are the key to every pass. Achieving good gates means a good #1 buoy, which sets you up for the rest of the pass. The secret to gates is consistently getting maximum leverage and lean at the right-hand gate buoy. You can achieve consistent gates by using a simple three-step process shown in figure 5.13. In phase A, you will learn the pullout. Next, in phase B, you will learn how to turn and lean through the gates. Finally, in phase C, you will learn the turn for the #1 buoy. When to make the turn, or the timing for the gates, is a separate subject that we will cover after we learn the perfect pullout, turn and lean, and #1 buoy.

Phase A: Pullout.   The pullout for the gates is like a golfer's address of a ball. You must do certain things to position yourself correctly for a good golf swing or a good gate shot. The pullout is where the slalom course begins, not at the gate buoys or the #1 buoy. You should begin from the left side of the wake and think of three things: making a smooth

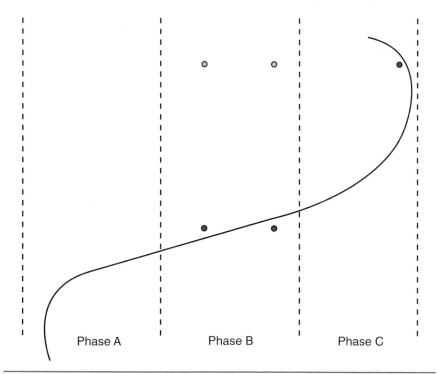

Phase A   Phase B   Phase C

Figure 5.13   Learning a consistent gate shot has three phases: the pullout (a), the turn and lean through the gates (b), and the turn for the #1 buoy (c).

controlled lean to the left; getting wide, up to at least the rear of the boat; and sinking into your ski by bending your knees and ankles as you begin your glide before the turn, as shown in figure 5.14.

Phase B: Turn and Lean.   When you are first learning the gates do not worry about going through them. In fact, I want you to miss them by 10 feet on the outside of the right gate buoy. We do this for two reasons. It makes it much easier to run the pass, and at this stage we are still working on mechanics in the course. You need to run as many successful passes as possible. The second reason is to learn the correct turn and lean. By concentrating on making the proper turn and lean, you will practice the good habits of leaning through the wakes rather than creating bad habits, such as letting up in your lean to go between the gate buoys. Refer to figure 5.13 to see the proper arc of the turn and where you would be crossing the wakes in relation to the gates. Figure 5.15 demonstrates the lean you need to get a good gate.

The perfect gate shot is one where you have your maximum angle and lean at the second wake and later at the right-hand gate buoy. Take this approach to attain the proper lean and angle. It will set you up wide and early for the #1 buoy, just as if you had pulled out to that side.

Figure 5.14   As you begin your glide before the turn to the gate, sink into your ski by bending your knees and ankles.

During your glide, as you settle into your ski, make a smooth rotation of your knees, hips, and shoulders toward the right side of the course. When the ski rotates through the turn, remember to stay low with your knees and let your arms out. This next stage is identical to the lean you use out of the #2 and #4 buoys. The lean should be pro-

Figure 5.15 Concentrating on making the proper turn and lean will help you develop the habit of leaning through the wakes rather than letting up as you go through the gate.

gressive and strong through the wakes. Concentrate on holding your direction across the course and pushing with your legs to create leverage against the boat. This part of the gates is the most critical. Too often I see skiers make a hard, fast turn and try to establish their maximum angle as quickly as possible. The results are always the same—the boat pulls them up at the second wake, and they ski straight and flat into the #1 buoy with a ton of speed. This scenario means a downcourse #1, and you are off chasing your tail the entire rest of the pass. When you make a hard, fast turn, you do establish your maximum angle, but too soon. The problem is that no one can hold that much angle to the second wake. When this happens, the skier's path looks like figure 5.16.

Phase C: #1 Buoy.   If you did things right in phases A and B, phase C is just as you have been doing all along. Make a smooth, controlled turn, get the handle back to your hips, and start your lean to #2. The reality of the situation is somewhat different. The distance from the gates to the #1 buoy is shorter than any other segment of the course. The key here becomes handle control—keeping the handle close to your body and in a low position near your hips. By doing this through the lean, you maintain your angle by keeping your shoulders and ski moving across course. The load, or pressure, forced on your ski will aid you in the edge change. The other part of handle control is holding on to the handle with both hands until you are into your turn. Good handle

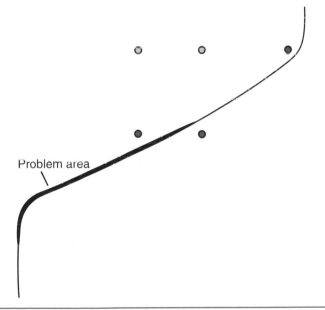

Problem area

Figure 5.16   If you make a hard, fast turn, you'll establish your maximum angle too soon.

control will get you skiing wide of the buoy so you are able to make your turn on the backside of the buoy. The turn should be a smooth, quick change of direction that sets you up for a powerful lean through the wakes to #2.

I stress the importance of learning how to perform the gate shot correctly. Even after you develop proper body position, you will not reach your goals if you cannot perform the gate shot correctly. Take the time to learn how to execute all three phases of the gate shot. It's not that difficult when you break it into A, B, and C. The key is to do all three correctly and consistently. Once you are doing the pullout, turn and lean, and #1 buoy properly, you are ready to attack the easy part of the gate shot—the timing.

To a certain extent you have already developed timing on your gate shot. When have you been starting your turn to miss the gates by 10 feet? That is timing—the when of the slalom course. When do you pull out? When do you turn and lean? The fact is that there is no magical rule or spot to go to. Every skier uses different reference points or sees things differently before the course. It is a trial-and-error process. The secret is *always* to do the same pullout, turn and lean, and #1 buoy. When you get a good #1 buoy make a mental note of where you started your pullout, turn, and so forth. You should focus on several things.

Figure 5.17   Your turn around #1 should be a smooth, quick change of direction that sets you up for a powerful lean through the wakes to #2.

1. Your target is to have your maximum angle at the right-hand gate buoy. You want your ski to be just inside that buoy. I instruct my students to focus their eyes like a laser beam on the right-hand buoy once they get into their glide.

2. It is difficult to maintain your angle and not let up to get between the gates. It may help if you aim for the middle of the right gate buoy, or two feet to its left. By doing this you will not let up to make it inside the gates. You will always be driving down to get closer to the right buoy. You are better off going through the middle of the gates with angle than being beside the right-hand buoy on a flat ski.

3. Use the distance between the boat and the gate buoy to give you a sense of when to start your pullout, turn, and so forth. Start by pulling out one boat length before the pregates (55-meter buoys) and turning as the nose of the boat goes through the gate buoys. (If your course does not have pregates, use another method to judge your pullout. The key is to be consistent.) Where were you? Did you miss the gates on the right side or did you go through the middle? If you missed them on the right, try coming downcourse in five-foot increments to get in the perfect location between the gate buoys. Do the opposite if you missed the gates on the left side or were too far from the right-hand buoy.

4. How the buoys line up in the course is another way to judge the timing for the gates. When the left gate buoy and #5 ball line up, begin your pullout. Keep pulling until you see the left-hand gate buoy and #3 ball line up. Go into your glide and begin your turn when the left-hand buoy and #1 buoy line up. I have found this method to be helpful since the course is the same at all sites.

Remember, the most important thing here is to have a consistent pullout and turn, and to hold your lean through the wakes. Play with the when factor, the timing, to adjust your gates.

BUILDING STRENGTH AND CONSISTENCY

The paradox of slalom is that you get to your hardest passes when you are the most tired. So a critical element of your slalom training is to prepare yourself so you still have maximum power and strength when you get to your most difficult pass. We must also make sure you get there often so you can press your limits and improve your scores. To do so, we must be patient and follow the B curve we discussed in chapter 1, spending time to develop and perfect our fundamentals. Before we start chasing scores, let's build a stronger foundation by doing these drills.

Drill 1: Back to Backs

Back to backs are simply starting at your opening pass and running it as many times as you can without stopping the boat. Spin the boat at the end of the course and come back in. When my coach, Jay Bennett, first instructed me to run back to backs, I did not see how running all those 28 and 32 off passes would help my high end passes at 38 and 39 off. It's boring, but it is the hardest workout you will ever do, and the benefits are innumerable. You build strength due to the volume, your consistency improves through the repetition, and your confidence rises because you learn to ski in any conditions and pull out of all sorts of bad situations.

Start off running two or three passes and build up. Set a goal for yourself or play a game with your training partner. We do both, especially in the winter and spring. My record for 32 off is 23 in a row without stopping the boat. I've heard rumors that Wade Cox has run fifteen 35 offs back to back. That's awesome! Make back to backs fun, because it is hard work. Remember that it pays dividends later. If you are serious about improving your skiing, you will do this drill.

Drill 2: Slow Skiing

This is a drill made famous by the slalom god of gods, Kris LaPoint. It teaches you flawless body position and the importance of pulling hard and strong through both wakes.

Run your first or second pass and stop the boat. Shorten the rope to 15 or 22 off, shorter if you are an advanced skier. Have the driver go through the course 2 mph slower than your normal speed. Spin the boat and come back in at another 2 mph slower. Keep doing this until you are going as slowly as you can. You will find that you must exaggerate everything—body position, lean, and so on—to make the pass. The smallest mistake puts you in the drink, so stay strong and work it.

Drill 3: Seven Buoy

What? You say there are only six buoys in your course? Imagine there is a seventh buoy. Make a turn at #6 just as you do at #2 and #4. Having the extra turn and lean keeps you from getting lazy at #5 or #6 and prevents the "I got this pass run" mentality from popping up because it's not over until you are around the #7 buoy. Turn #7 and go back through the pregates if you have them.

Drill 4: Two-Handing

Now that you are a veteran slalom course skier and are making perfect sweeping one-hand reaches and turns, try to run a pass with two hands on the handle in the turns as you did when you were first learning. It's harder than you may think. This is one of my favorite training drills. It breaks up the turn and lean into separate phases and teaches you handle control. Steve Schnitzer, several times a national champion and an innovative slalom ski designer, is the best two-hander I've ever seen. Schnitz is an amazing technical skier. I've seen him run 38 off two-handed. A few pointers for this drill are to keep your chest up in the turn and the ski in front of you by staying down in your ski. Second, finish the turn, and then make a strong lean. This is where you make up time, and this drill will teach you how to get across the wakes quickly. Third, reach with your outside hand. Begin by slowing the boat 2 mph the first time you try two-handing. Build back up and see how far you can go.

Advanced Slalom Theory

The key to slalom theory is the pendulum effect. You are the weight at the end of a pendulum staff that moves back and forth. The physics of slalom is very similar. You must maintain your angle and direction through the wakes and into the edge change by keeping your shoulders

Figure 5.18   Running a pass with both hands on the handle will teach you handle control.

traveling across the course, rather than letting them rotate back toward the boat. This may feel as if it gives you a burst of speed off the second wake. That's OK. This extra resistance at the second wake will allow you to carry your ski out wider of the buoy and will slow you down so you finish the turn on the backside of the buoy. You must ski wide of the buoy or you will carry too much speed in the turn. By finishing the turn at the buoy, you move farther up on the side of the boat and get into the acceleration and lean phase sooner. The sooner you lean, the quicker you will get to the other side of the course and the earlier you will be at the next buoy. If you feel as if you are narrow or late in the slalom course, think wide and employ the pendulum effect.

The second part of slalom theory is learning to ski early. When you nail that turn and get the great feeling of angle on the backside of the buoy, the temptation is to look across the course, see how early you are going to be, and forget the lean. I call this skiing lazy. Learn to suppress the elation that comes from a great turn; there is still much work to do. Take all that angle you have created and turn it into acceleration as quickly as possible to get to the other side of the course. Pull your hardest through the wakes and behind the boat as shown in figure 5.19 because in this situation you have the correct direction and angle. This will position you up on the boat farther and prevent the boat from pulling you forward in the turn.

If you feel as if you are being pulled forward, you are behind the boat in the turn. When you fail to attain your angle out of the turn, you still need to pull your hardest as quickly as you can, as shown in figure 5.20. You

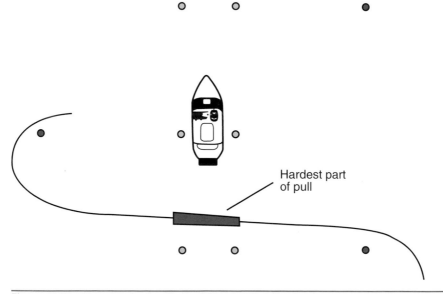

Figure 5.19   Your hardest pull should be behind the boat.

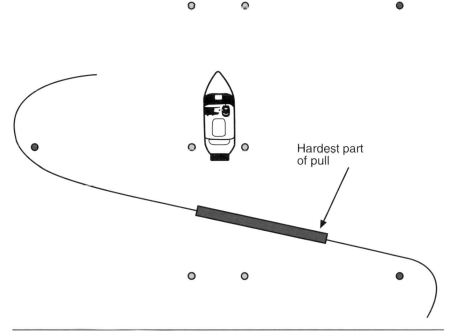

Figure 5.20   If you don't have the right angle out of the turn, you can still create angle before the wakes by pulling your hardest as quickly as you can.

still have a chance to create angle before the wakes since you are still up on the boat a bit, so get your shoulders rotated and lean. In this situation, you need to pull your hardest as soon as you get both hands back on the handle, before the first wake. You must then maintain your pull and angle through the wakes and be patient at the next buoy because you will still be a little narrow and a little fast. The good news is that you have another chance to make up time in the next pull. Don't try to run a pass with one turn or pull—stay in the pass and on your ski. Work with the pass and never give up.

ADVANCED SLALOM

The advanced slalom skier is the toughest to coach. We started chapter 3 by commenting on how many skiers have spent hours or even years skiing and training based on the folklore of what top skiers are supposedly saying, doing, or teaching. The problem is that what top skiers are working on or teaching is for them, or their student, not you. Yes, the theories and technical aspects are the same, but you may be wasting your time working on a drill or technique that does not apply to a problem area for you. The secret to learning that next pass is to go about it in an organized manner, not just try this drill once and that technique twice and maybe another approach a few times. In this section we will provide a framework for you to use in learning that next line length. We will also reveal the mystery of how to tune your slalom ski. I invite the advanced skier to invoke the beginner's mind we talked about in chapter 1. Take the time to read the beginner and intermediate sections of this chapter if you skipped them. You will find drills that the top skiers use in training and coaching. Back up and do these drills if you don't already use them in training. They will help you attain your goals more quickly, and the information will make you a better coach for your ski partner and friends.

Skill 1: Learning the Next Pass

It is a feeling of personal triumph when you run the slalom course for the first time. You come out of the gates and throw up the iron fist. The feeling is addictive. The adrenaline thrusts through you like the space shuttle blasting off to outer space. You want to have that feeling again, except this time it will be more intense because the boat is going faster or the rope is shorter. You try and try, but nothing works. You are getting slack at the #1 ball, you can't get the gates right, you aren't getting into a lean, you keep over turning. Stop! You need a system that makes that new pass runnable. Here are four ways to help you to learn a new pass.

1. The most difficult part of learning a new pass is adjusting to the change in the pull from the boat. As the rope gets shorter, the pull is quicker and much more intense. The gates become even more critical and difficult to time. The best way to learn a new pass is the same way you learned your first pass—by ignoring the gates. Break each new pass into two sections: the rhythm of the pass and the gate shot. You should first learn the rhythm. Time your turn and lean through the gates so you miss them by five feet on the right side of the #1 buoy. This will position you wide on the #1 buoy and give you ample time to slow down to make a nice, smooth turn on the backside of the buoy. Now you are off and running the pass. From there on it is simply learning the rhythm of the pass and how to hold the additional stress of the pull from the boat.

The next phase is learning the gates. You can run the pass by missing the gates by five feet, so now do the same thing but miss them by two feet, as shown in figure 5.21. As always, the trick is holding your lean and angle through the gates and getting the whip out to the buoy. Once you can run the pass from a two-foot-miss position, go for it. You will fall and have problems. Stay focused. You know you can run the pass once you get started. Often you will get the perfect gate and #1 buoy but fall at #2 or #3. Stay calm. What happens is that you come to #2 and you are still thinking about that awesome gate and the #1 buoy rather

Figure 5.21   After you can run a new pass missing the gates, start learning the gates for the pass by missing them by two feet.

than what you need to be thinking at #2. Just like that you are in the lake. Once you develop consistency on the gate, the pass will be a snap. To get to that level, break the pass up into the rhythm and the gate shot.

2. When you are learning that next pass it will feel as if the boat is moving much faster. It's not. As the rope gets shorter, the physics of slalom requires you to travel a greater distance in the same amount of time. The shorter the rope, the quicker things happen in the course. You need to edge change quicker, turn quicker, get into your lean quicker. So you need to go faster even though the boat does not. You will usually run that new pass with a slow boat time before you make the pass with a regulation time because you are accustomed to that slower speed. One method to prepare for this increased acceleration is first to run the passes you are currently making at faster speeds, say a quarter to a half mile per hour faster. Those small increases in speed make things happen more quickly, and the pull is a bit stronger as well, requiring more leverage and lean. This will sharpen you mentally for the speed at which things will be happening. To ensure success when you do cut the rope, slow the boat 1 mph. Once you make the pass gates and all at the slower speed, gradually bump the speed up to tolerance.

3. Some drivers will weave the boat to help a skier stretching to make a new pass. I don't like this method. Driving is hard enough, and when you weave things are even more inconsistent. I prefer a midloop. Do one of two things. Either fid a new loop into your rope between the pass you are currently running and the new pass or wrap the rope around the pylon a few times to ease the difference. Either way, the change won't be as dramatic, and you will gain confidence and have a smooth transition into the new pass.

4. You must learn to trust your edge change. After 22 off things begin to shift. The pulls are stronger and quicker, and things happen much faster, but the biggest modification is adapting to the visual change. No longer can you pull until your head is outside the buoy. As Schnitz says, you have to start "trusting your edge change." When you complete your lean, you must trust that your ski will carry out and around the next buoy even though at first it may not look as if it will make it. Figure 5.22 demonstrates this concept. A common mistake people make when they get into that new pass is waiting for a turn until it looks like 15 off. I

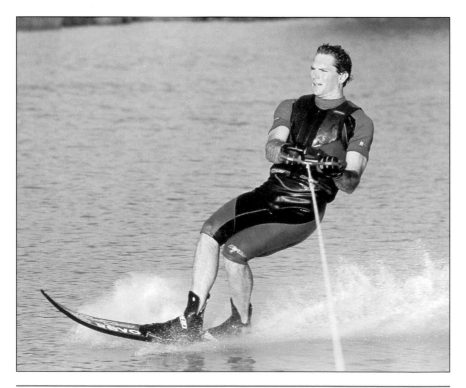

Figure 5.22   After 22 off, you have to learn to trust your edge change. When you finish your pull, change direction and get back across the course.

challenge you to make a good, strong pull through the wakes and try to turn before the buoy. I have never had a student who could get the ski turned before the buoy if he or she made a true pull and held their angle. The point is that as soon as you finish your pull, change direction and get back across the course. If you wait for the buoy, you will be downcourse and losing angle. Be aggressive and get across course quickly.

I have one last tip for short-line slalom. A few years back the top pros began to use new slalom styles. An alternative to the traditional style epitomized by Lucky Lowe is the newer compression style being used by Andy Mapple and Wade Cox. Both styles are great. The key is finding which style fits the way you ski. The traditional style is more locked out and rigid, with the back arched and the handle pinned to the hip. The skier rides slightly higher in the ski and has considerably less knee and ankle flexion in the turns and through the wakes. With the compression style, the skier is much lower in the ski, especially out of the turn. The handle is farther away from the body, but the skier maintains leverage by pressing with the legs and dropping away from the rope. Both styles have good and bad points. I prefer the newer style because it is more forgiving in rough water. Also, you have more room for error because you are less exposed to the boat out of the turn. I'm sure Lucky would effectively argue the point for his style, in his friendly Alabama drawl, and he wouldn't be wrong. The traditional style uses your maximum body leverage and is less dependent on strength. There is less jerking and yanking from the boat, and the rhythm is smooth and consistent with locked-out pulls and arcing turns. Either way, get a video of Lucky, Andy, or Wade, notice the style differences, and try to find a style that fits you.

BUYING AND TUNING YOUR SLALOM SKI

Few skiers ever find the right balance for their equipment setup. It seems most skiers are stuck on the extremes of the continuum. Either they spend nearly 100 percent of their time fiddling with fin settings or ski adjustments, or they are scared to touch their ski setup for fear of losing what feels good. The problem with not trying new skis or settings is that you never know if there is a better ski for you or if there is a better setup that will help you overcome your faults. Try these tips for selecting a ski and setting it up to advance your skiing scores.

Selecting a New Ski

Go to your local pro shop and try several demo skis before you buy. To determine which skis to try, mismatch your strengths and weaknesses. If you have great turns and poor pulls, try skis that are known for getting across the wakes with good angle. If you are a bull across the wakes but have trouble slowing down and turning, try skis with better deceleration and turning characteristics. The idea is to improve your weaknesses. Getting on a ski that feels the same as your old one gets you only newer graphics. Rate each ski on turning, acceleration, deceleration, and how it maintains angle across the wakes. Ask yourself what each ski you try does differently, better and worse, from your current ski. Make a decision based on those answers, not on the colors or price.

Once you find a ski that you like and works for you, spend a few sets adjusting to it before making any setup changes. When you are comfortable riding the ski and know what it is doing, begin fine-tuning the setup. Start with the bindings, then the fin, and as a last measure take out the file or sandpaper to dial it in. This is where you must carefully track each change. Make only one change at a time, and take notes on what you changed and how it affected the ski's performance. Make sure you are not inadvertently causing problems by skiing lazy or tired. Remember, every adjustment will improve one aspect of the ski's performance, but only at the cost of making another characteristic less than perfect. Once you get into the season, have confidence in your setup and know what you are doing before you fall into the overtuning trap.

Tuning Your Ski

Nine design elements determine the personality or performance characteristics of a slalom ski. A change in any of these factors totally changes the attitude of the ski and affects the attributes and performance of other components. Remember that no one ski design is the best. You must find a ski that works for you and helps you overcome your particular technical flaws. Everything in ski design is a trade-off. To increase one characteristic, you decrease another. You must find what works for you through experimentation and trial and error. To help you do so efficiently, here is an explanation of each of the nine ski adjustments or personality factors, the effects they have on a ski, and how to tune or adjust them.

Bottom Design.   Manufacturers use three designs. Try different tunnel designs to find one that matches the way you ski or the way you want a ski to perform.

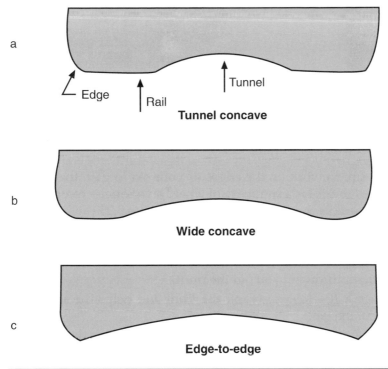

Figure 5.23   Bottom designs: (a) tunnel concave, (b) wide concave, (c) edge-to-edge concave.

Tunnel concave—Narrow, concave tunnels are more stable and track better. If the rails are angled toward the bevel, the ski will roll on edge easier. Rails provide lift and stability.

Wide concave—Wide concave skis sit deeper, change edges easier, and are less stable on the water. Deeper concave skis decelerate and hold better. Shallower concave skis cause the ski to ride higher on the water, making them easier to turn.

Edge-to-edge—Edge-to-edge concave skis, if the same depth as a constant-radius concave ski, have more surface area in the tunnel and therefore more suction and holding power.

Edge Shape.   Little has been said or written about this topic since the 1982 *Water Skier* article "How to Tune a Slalom Ski" by Dave Saucier (see table 5.1). This article is still the edge tuner's bible. You can change a lot by working edges, so proceed with caution before you start filing. We will explain the two types of bevels used today and give some tips on edge tuning.

45-degree bevel—Sharp edges lift the ski higher, resulting in less drag and less spray. The ski rides as if it is on a track or rail. The greater the size of the bevel, the farther the ski will drop into the water, resulting in a steadier ride with more drag. The rounder the bevel, the more the ski will drop into the water, and the easier it will roll from edge to edge.

Modified 45-degree bevel—The ski will sit deeper in the water than with a straight 45-degree bevel, resulting in a ski that is easier to turn but does not track as well. The smaller the bevel, the higher the ski will ride on the water. See figure 5.24.

If you desire to work on the edges of your ski to gain that performance edge, table 5.1 is a summary of what Dave Saucier recommends for each of the ski's three zones as shown in figure 5.25.

Perimeter Shape.   The following are perimeter shapes.

Wide forebody—Allows you to stand on the front of the ski to carve a turn without throwing you out the front.

Narrow forebody—Keeps you off the front and helps the ski turn if you are on the tail.

Wide tail—Offers better acceleration if you tend to ride the tail of the ski.

Narrow tail—Slows down more quickly and rides deeper in the water.

Wide midsection—Turns more easily because the ski will pivot on the flat section.

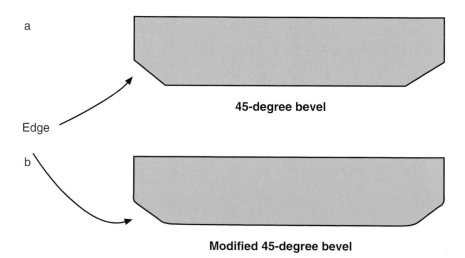

Figure 5.24   Edge shapes: (a) 45-degree bevel, (b) modified 45-degree bevel.

Table 5.1   Troubleshooting Chart
(assuming bindings are properly located)

Trouble	Zone	Soften	Sharpen	Bot. edge	Side edge
			Solution		
Ski lifts excessively over wake	1, 2	x		x	
Ski shifts edges slowly	2	x		x	
Ski is slow getting into preturn braking	2	x		x	
Ski lacks preturn aggression (preturn radius too large) during braking and extension	3	x		x	
Ski dumps too quickly (causes breaking at waist)	3		x		x
Ski dumps before pull-in and weight shift starts	3		x		x
Ski tip dives on bad side during washout	3[a]		x		x
Ski tip *chatters* during dump and washout	3		x		x
Ski lacks aggression during dump and washout. Lays you down or requires excess body angle to get into proper acceleration path	2[b]	x		x	
Ski lacks track on acceleration. Does not carve into wake	1[c]		x		x
Ski shoots out of course approaching bad side turn. Actually turns wrong way as you start preturn (hard fall)	3[d]	x		x	
Ski walks or hunts from one side to another when going straight ahead; i.e., it wiggles	2[e]				
Ski rides too high out of water overall	1, 2[f]	x		x	
Ski rides at too shallow angle to direction of travel; i.e., tail is too high, tip too low	1	x		x	
Lack of preturn braking coming around buoy into slack line even though you are in correct path	2	x		x	

(continued)

Table 5.1 *(continued)*

Trouble	Zone	Solution Soften	Sharpen	Bot. edge	Side edge
Ski tends to *bounce* as it lands off wake; tends to *rebound* (two possible zones; two possible solutions)	1, 2	x	x	x	x*
Ski jets out from under skier at 4th, 5th cuts (check binding location for being back too far or for ski being too short for skier's weight)	1	x Greatly		x Just at fin area	
Ski seems slow on acceleration; i.e., attack angle too shallow	2	x			x

*Forward part only.
Notes: [a]Possibly slightly wider bevel in this area.
[b]Favor point in between feet.
[c]Expecially at fin area.
[d]Soften tunnel edges also full length.
[e]Zone of demarcation between two edges must be established; i.e., two edges have been softened into each other. Also check binding location. Bindings back too far (2"-3") cause this.
[f]Also increase bevel width and re-edge (both zones).

a

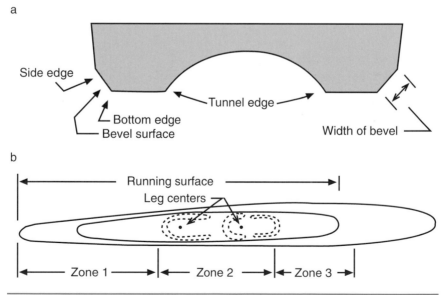

Side edge

Tunnel edge

Bottom edge
Bevel surface

Width of bevel

b

Running surface

Leg centers

Zone 1   Zone 2   Zone 3

Figure 5.25   Edge areas (a) and zones (b) for edge tuning.
Table 5.1 and figure 5.25 from "How to tune a slalom ski," 1992, *Water Skier* (Winter Haven, FL: American Water Ski Association).

Side Cut.   Three types of side cuts:

Sharp pivot point—Allows the ski to turn more sharply given the same weight distribution.

Medium—Combines pivot and smooth perimeter shape.

Smooth—Has no abrupt pivot point, just a smooth, rounded perimeter.

Rocker.   Ski companies are beginning to do more testing with rocker patterns. You can bet that they will soon be introducing adjustable tail rocker devices. Figure 5.26 shows two basic rocker patterns:

Continuous—Turns more easily when weight distribution is on the tail.

Flat section—Is more stable, accelerates better, and allows for a forward weight distribution. This type of rocker pattern has a distinct tail with more rocker, as seen in figure 5.26b. The more rocker in the tail, the easier it is to turn but the slower the acceleration. The less the tail rocker, the harder it is to turn but the faster the acceleration.

Flex.   Flex, which works in conjunction with rocker, is the variable that the new Flex Plates (figure 5.27a) and Power Stix (5.27b) are attempting to adjust. In general terms, the flatter the ski, the softer the ski can be. The ski with more rocker needs less flex. However, the Flex Plates and Power Stix give you control of flex and flex response time as well as a slight degree of rocker adjustment. Changes to these devices will yield the following outcomes.

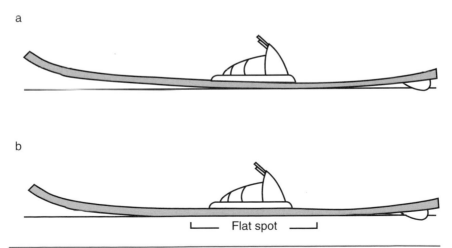

a

b

Flat spot

Figure 5.26   Slalom ski rocker patterns: (a) continuous and (b) flat section.

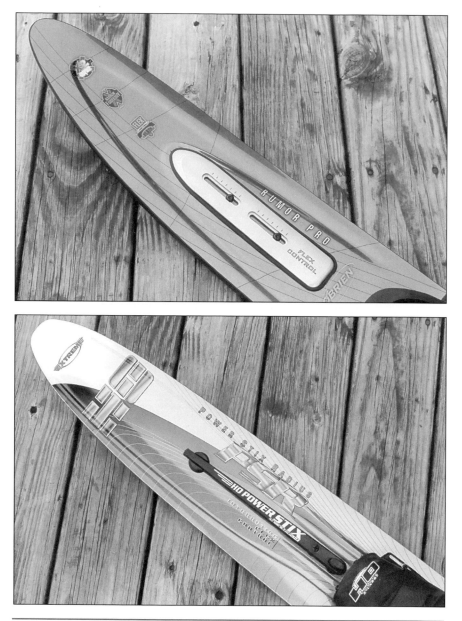

Figure 5.27   Flex Plate (a) and Power Stix (b).

Loosening the Flex Plate or Power Stix or skis with soft flex patterns—The easier the ski is to turn, the more forgiving the ski. You will have more time before the ski shoots you across the wakes.

Tightening the Flex Plate or Power Stix or skis with stiff flex patterns— The harder it is to turn, the better the acceleration.

Both of these flex devices dampen ski vibration, or chatter, and reduce the flex recovery time, making the ski accelerate more quickly.

Fin Shapes and Adjustments. The following are different kinds of fin shapes and adjustments.

Fins with flatter leading edges (left fins in figure 5.28) cause the front of the ski to stay up, resulting in more speed in the turn. They require more force to finish the turn.

Rounded-radius, leading-edge fins (right fins in figure 5.28) drive the front of the ski into the water. They start the turn sooner and finish with more ski in the water.

Square or straight-tail fins (bottom fins in figure 5.28) allow the skier to push harder on the ski during the on side, but require more effort on the off side to finish the turn.

Rounded-back fins (top fins in figure 5.28) will have more tail slide on the off side but may be too much slide on the on side.

I have found that skiers tend to ski a fin shape as much as they do a ski. Try several different shapes until you find one that fits your style. Once you settle on a shape, think about fine-tuning the fin with these adjustments. You can adjust the fin in three ways.

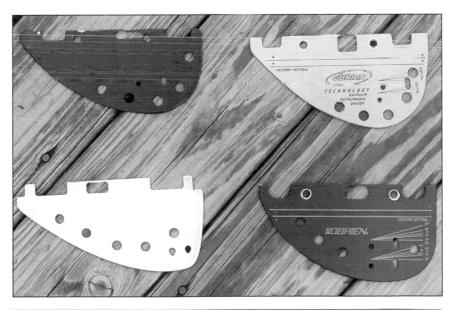

Figure 5.28 Fin shapes: fins with flatter leading edges (left fins); rounded-radius leading-edge fins (right fins); square or straight-tail fins (bottom fins); and rounded-back fins (top fins).

Horizontal adjustment—Moving the fin forward toward the ski tip or backward toward the tail (figure 5.29a) controls the front of the ski on the on-side turn. A forward adjustment will lift the front of the ski and drop the tail. A backward adjustment will drive the front of the ski into the water.

Vertical adjustment—Moving the fin up toward the top of the ski and down in the direction of the ski bottom controls turning stability, ease, and holding power for both on- and off-side turns (figure 5.29b). By moving the fin up you will make it easier to turn and increase tail slide. A downward adjustment will increase stability and reduce tail slide yet make it harder to turn.

Diagonal adjustment—A diagonal adjustment either increases or decreases the leading-edge length and controls the off-side turn (figure 5.29c). A longer, fuller leading edge drives the front of the ski into the water, making for a quicker, more aggressive turn. A shorter leading edge raises the front of the ski, resulting in a longer, rounded turn.

Binding Location.   The first adjustment to look at is binding position. I recommend the binding location set at the factory, but there is always the temptation to move them forward or backward a notch or two. Some people will drill new holes in the ski to get the bindings to a location they feel will work. The on-side turn (buoys #2, #4, #6 for right-foot-forward skiers and buoys #1, #3, #5 for left-foot-forward skiers) is controlled by your rear foot. The off-side turn is controlled by the front foot. How do binding location changes affect performance?

Forward—If you need quicker deceleration and tighter turns, move forward. You are too far forward if you ski narrow and reach forward.

Backward—If you need better acceleration or more controlled turns, move backward. You are too far back if the ski will not slow down or if you have to put excessive weight on your front foot to slow it down.

Wing Adjustments.   Ski tuning is not complete without understanding the effects of the wing. Different sizes and shapes have impact on ski performance, but the primary purpose of the wing is to aid in slowing the ski before the turn and stabilizing the ski in the preturn.

Higher on the ski—Provides more deceleration and braking. The ski also rolls up on edge more because of an increase in tip pressure on your on-side turn.

Lower on the ski—Provides more stability through the wakes and in the turns. The ski will turn better on your off-side turn because of the increase in tip pressure.

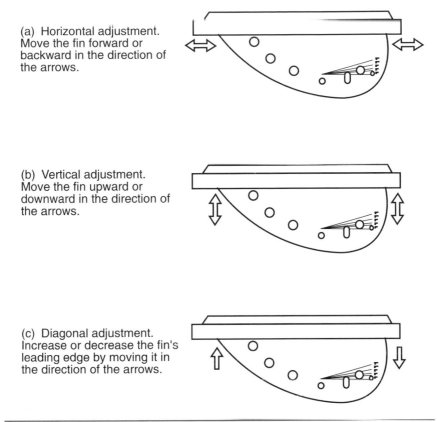

(a) Horizontal adjustment. Move the fin forward or backward in the direction of the arrows.

(b) Vertical adjustment. Move the fin upward or downward in the direction of the arrows.

(c) Diagonal adjustment. Increase or decrease the fin's leading edge by moving it in the direction of the arrows.

Figure 5.29 Fin adjustments: (a) horizontal, (b) vertical, and (c) diagonal.

Increase wing angle—Increases drag and slows the ski more quickly.

Decrease wing angle—Allows you to carry more speed through the turn.

The combinations are endless. You could spend the rest of your life searching for the elusive perfect setting. Be careful not to fall into the overtuning trap. There are so many variables to adjust that it is easy to lose sight of the fundamentals of good slalom skiing. Adjust one thing at a time. Track your performances and settings with a tuning log such as the one shown in on page 111. Find a setting that is consistent and feels comfortable. Spend your time working on the fundamentals of good body position and gate shots. When you ski poorly, evaluate yourself first. Odds are that *you* changed more than the ski did. Once you find a setting that works for you, do not change it to gain a certain desirable characteristic unless you understand what you will give up in return.

ADJUSTING A FIN

Problem: Breaking at the waist during off-side turn.

Solution: Make a diagonal adjustment by moving front of fin up into the ski.

Problem: Ski will not initiate on turns on both on and off sides.

Solution: Make a horizontal adjustment by moving the entire fin forward toward the front of the ski, or make a vertical adjustment by moving the entire fin up into the ski.

Problem: Ski tip riding high or out of the water in on-side turn.

Solution: Make a horizontal adjustment by moving the entire fin backward toward the tail of the ski.

Problem: Ski tip biting or too much in the water during on-side turn.

Solution: Make a horizontal adjustment by moving entire fin forward toward the front of the ski.

(continued)

Problem: Edge change is too slow. Ski makes long, slow downcourse turns. Front of the ski comes out of the water at the end of the turn on either side.

Solution: Make a vertical adjustment by moving entire fin up into the ski, reducing the fin depth, or make a horizontal adjustment by moving entire fin forward toward the front of the ski.

Problem: Ski is too responsive or edgy. Tail of the ski slides around in the turn. Tail washes out or blows out at the end of the turn.

Solution: Make a vertical adjustment by moving entire fin down out of the ski, increasing the fin depth, or make a horizontal adjustment by moving entire fin backward toward the tail of the ski.

SKI TUNING AND ADJUSTMENT LOG

Date: _____

Ski name or model: _____

Design specifications:

Flex: Overall _____   _____

           Tip   _____   _____

           Mid   _____   _____ Special

           Tail   _____   _____ layup

                                                        pattern

Rocker: Overall _____   _____

           Tip   _____   _____

           Tail   _____   _____

Adjustments	Current setting	New setting	Reason for change	Expected results	Score
Binding location					
Fin: Shape Length Depth Front/back					
Wing: Angle Location					
Edge modification					

Notes, comments, things to try next:

_____

_____

_____

_____

_____

_____

_____

CHAPTER 6

TRICK SKIING, WAKEBOARDING, AND KNEEBOARDING

I'm sure I'll catch heat from traditional trickers, diehard kneeboarders, and wakeboarding purists by combining these three events. They will say I don't understand the essence of their particular event and the radical differences among them. Yes, there are differences, but those differences are primarily in how the event is performed in competition, not in how you land the tricks. I have grouped these three disciplines together for a couple of reasons. First, from an instructional viewpoint, you can learn tricks on any type of ski or board more quickly by using a natural learning progression. I will use the word "tricks" as a generic term to describe the maneuver being performed, but the type of equipment can be any of the three. Second, the fundamentals of performing most beginner and intermediate tricks are basically the same. Whether you are doing a 360 helicopter on a trick ski, wakeboard, or kneeboard, you use similar basic skills.

The real test of your fundamental skills is tricking and boarding. Don't let this intimidate you. These events challenge your balance, edge control, pressure control, and turning ability more than any other event. They are also the easiest events to become involved with, and you can quickly learn new tricks if you build a solid foundation. Tricking and boarding offer an advantage over slalom and jumping because no courses or jumps are required. You can do the tricks anywhere, and usually in any water conditions. You ski at much slower speeds, which saves money on gas and requires a less powerful boat. The slow speed also makes these events less painful when you take a plunge. You will also improve in your other events by learning how to ride trick skis or boards. As we mentioned, performing tricks forces you to develop excellent balance, strong pressure and edge control, and smooth turning skills. Controlling the forces of the boat and water demands precise execution and body position. By acquiring awareness of your body in space, you become a better skier overall. Another benefit of tricking and boarding is that they are a great change of pace and won't wear out your hands and body as slalom does. So let's turn some heads with flips, twists, and turns.

BASIC SKILLS AND TRICKS

To start, let's discuss basic two-ski skills and tricks. You perform the kneeboard versions exactly as you do the two-ski versions, but from a kneeling position. After learning basic body position and riding drills, the wakeboard basics are more similar to the one-ski tricks and skills, so we will cover them later in this chapter.

Rising out of the water on two trick skis is done just as you do it on two skis. This is where things get a bit slippery. Trick skis and kneeboards have no fins to stabilize them, so they are more difficult to control, and you may need a few tries before you become comfortable. Everyone learning to trick takes the same goofy falls. Take your time and develop the patience you will need to become an accomplished tricker. Our first goal is to learn to ride the trick skis or boards with correct body position and control. Once we get that down, we will begin learning the basic two-ski tricks. Getting up on a kneeboard or wakeboard for the first time is usually a bit easier than getting up on trick skis. As you see in figure 6.1, on a kneeboard you start by lying on the board and pulling yourself up to your knees as the board planes off.

Wakeboarding is somewhat easier because of the fins on the board. Start with the board cocked to the side, your knees to your chest, and your arms straight. The board will slide sideways for a moment, then straighten out. Figure 6.2 shows how you must stay in a crouched position until the board is straight. It may be easier to learn how to trick ski if you first take a ride on a kneeboard or wakeboard.

Figure 6.1 Kneeboard start.

Skill 1: Body Position

In the slalom chapter we talked about the value of dry-land practice. Well, for these events, dry-land practice is about 10 times more important. The *AWSA Coaches Manual* says dry-land practice is essential, and I agree. Save yourself and your boat crew time and frustration by learning every trick on land before taking it to the water. To get a good simulation of the pull and how you must advance on the boat to perform a trick, set up a simple pulley system on the dock or at home (figure 6.3). Or at least tie a handle to a tree to practice the required movements. If you don't, you will end up taking hundreds of unnecessary falls.

Figure 6.2   Wakeboard start.

Rope approx. 10 ft
Height of pulley approx. 3½ ft

Weight: 10-20 lb

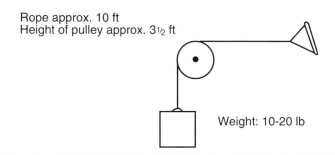

Figure 6.3   Set up a simple pulley system and practice tricks on land before taking them to the water.

The first thing to practice on land is body position. Using a mirror can be helpful in checking your position. Take a close look at figures 6.4, 6.5, and 6.6. What do you notice? All the skiers, whether on trick skis, kneeboard, or wakeboard, are in similar positions.

Knees and ankles bent (on trick skis and wakeboard), back straight, handle held with both palms down at waist height, and head and eyes on the horizon is the correct body position. You can't tell in the photo, but the skier's weight is centered over the skis and board. Imitate this position on land and then take it to the water.

Because trick skis have no fins, they are difficult to track and edge at first. To help improve the tracking and control of the skis, keep your speed slow, about 11 to 15 mph for an average-size adult. In learning to ride your trick skis or board, you should practice and be comfortable with several skills before trying any tricks. Focus on body position while doing these drills.

Edging With Angulation.   Learn to edge the skis or board and pop off the wake. You edge with angulation as shown in figure 6.7. Notice the low position and flex of the ankles and knees as they push the hips

Figure 6.4   Body position for trick skiing.

Figure 6.5   Body position for wakeboarding.

Figure 6.6   Body position for kneeboarding.

Figure 6.7   Learn to edge through the wakes.

toward the direction of the wake. Edge all the way to the top of the wake and extend your legs while keeping your upper body still and shoulders level with the water's surface. This is different from jumping on land, so keep at it until you can nearly jump both wakes.

Advancing on the Boat.   To perform tricks, you must break free from the forward pull of the boat by advancing on the boat or rope. Do this by progressively pulling stronger on the rope. The strongest pull should be at the end of the inward pull. Make sure you maintain proper body position. This drill teaches what is known as handle control. Handle control is extremely important in tricking, so take your time to learn these relatively simple skills.

Skill 2: Basic Two-Ski Tricks

Basic two-ski tricks are the side slide, front to back, back to front, front to front, and the wake and reverse versions of these tricks. Hit the water only after going through each trick on land.

Side Slide.   This is the first trick that trickers and kneeboarders should learn. (This trick is more difficult for wakeboarders because of the fins on the board.) The side slide teaches balance, control of the rope and handle, and the body position that underlies all tricks. The process of performing this trick follows: Establish solid body position. Make a firm, even pull on the rope in to the waist. Turn the skis or board 90 degrees with your knees, hips, and shoulders. It may help to let go with one hand and turn in the direction of your free hand. Keep the handle at your waist and maintain an upright position during the turn, as shown in figure 6.8. The knees must remain soft and flexible during the turn. Keep the skis spread slightly for stability and the free arm extended for balance. The most common fall is having the skis slip out during the turn, which is caused by leaning away from the boat. To correct this, center your weight over the skis by bending your ankles and resting your weight on the balls of your feet.

Figure 6.8   The side slide is the first trick that trick skiers and kneeboarders should learn.

Front to Back.   You show-offs out there will begin to turn heads with this trick. The back, as it is called, is simply a continuation of the side slide, except that you complete the rotation to a 180-degree turn. You will get some looks from those in other boats when they see you cruising down the lake backward. This trick is much easier to do on a kneeboard, and doing so will teach you the pull and rotation. So before going to the trick skis or wakeboard, try it on a kneeboard. Begin from your basic position and pull in the rope firmly and smoothly to the hip opposite the direction you are going to turn. Begin the turn by completing the pull-in, releasing with the hand away from the boat, and leading the turn with the hips. Keep the handle close to your waist and turn the skis or board backward. Grab the handle with the free hand and press it into the small of the back, just above your rear. Once skiing backward, maintain body position identical to forward position as shown in figure 6.9. Keep knees bent, back straight, handle in to the waist, body leaning away from the boat slightly, and head and eyes up. Some may have success doing this trick before the side slide; do whatever feels more natural to you.

Back to Front.   Now that you are skiing backward, it's time to turn around again and see where you are going. The front is done by simply letting go with one hand and keeping the handle in to the waist without letting the arm extend out away from the body. Figure 6.10 demonstrates how you need to keep your chest up as you rotate forward to maintain your vertical axis. Grab the handle with the free hand and complete the rotation. The key is keeping the handle close to the body and learning to pull on the rope from the back position.

Reverse Back and Front.   Once you can do these tricks turning in the direction that is natural for you, don't waste time. Learn the same trick in the opposite direction. These tricks are known as reverses. If you aspire to be a good tricker, you can't avoid the reverse tricks. Begin now to get the feeling of turning the opposite way. Although you do the trick the same way, it may take longer to learn because you are not as strong or confident turning to the other side. Don't think about it. You know how to do it—just go out there and land it on your first try.

Front to Front.   We have talked extensively about learning progression. Progression is extremely important in tricking and boarding, and the front to front (or 360) demonstrates why. The key to the 360 is dividing it into two 180s—a front to back followed by a back to front in the same direction. We will learn all multiple-rotation tricks by breaking them down into their basic tricks. Begin by doing a back, stopping, and

Figure 6.9   Front to back.

holding the position for a moment. Now do a front in the same direction. Keep doing this, but pause more briefly each time. A few pointers for the smooth, credited version of this trick follow:

Figure 6.10   Back to front.

1. Make a slightly stronger pull in on the rope than you do for a 180.
2. Make a smooth exchange of the handle and keep it close to the body.
3. On trick skis or a wakeboard, keep your knees soft and flexible.
4. Maintain correct body position throughout the trick, keep your head up with your eyes focused on the horizon, and make smooth, continuous movements.

Basic Wake Tricks.   To do a wake trick properly, you must perform the trick in the air, with the skis not touching the water's surface. The wake-jumping drill we described earlier will pay off here. If you have taken the time to learn how to edge up the wake and get the lift the wake provides, these tricks will be a breeze. If not, go back and learn how to jump the wakes and edge the trick skis or board with angulation to feel the top of the wake. You may find it easier to do the wake tricks by sliding the tricks over the wake at first. Although you don't get any air on the trick, you learn how to edge and pull at the same time. After successfully sliding the tricks, take a more aggressive edge and push off the wake's crest as you pull the handle in to your hip and begin the rotation.

Do the wake version of the back, front, and reverses just as you did the basic version. You begin from the middle of the wakes or about three feet outside the wake, edge up and through the wake, and push off the wake at the crest. Use the wake on the side to which you are turning—the right wake for a clockwise turn and the left wake for a counterclockwise rotation. If you are having trouble slipping out as you land the trick, get in a lower position on the ski or board by flexing your ankles and knees and dropping your hip into the wake. Also try arching your back more to keep your head and chest up and in line with your rotational axis.

TROUBLESHOOTING BASIC TRICKS

Three falls commonly occur when learning basic tricks.

FALL: Away from the boat as you turn.

Error: Looking down.
Solution: Focus eyes on the tops of the trees. Keep head and shoulders up.

FALL: Toward the boat in a backward position.

Error: Ankles and knees too stiff.
Solution: Stress the knee and ankle bend. Get weight on toes as you turn and maintain position.

FALL: Forward when only halfway through turn.

Error: Not advancing on boat enough, or allowing handle to leave your waist during turn.
Solution: Make a strong, smooth pull on the rope.

To develop a solid foundation, you should learn each wake trick in both the basic and reverse rotation from inside to outside the wake, outside to inside, and off both wakes. If you do a wake trick and the reverse off both wakes and in both directions, you have a total of eight ways to perform each wake trick. This is a great drill to prepare you for more advanced tricks.

TRANSITIONAL TRICKS AND TIPS

As stated earlier, trick skiing has evolved dramatically in the last several years. More high-tech equipment is available, and skiers are performing more difficult types of tricks. In the 1980s only the top skiers were doing flips, and only a handful of them did body overs and ski line tricks. Most tricking was wake turns and toe turns. Part of this evolution is the result of kids wanting to do cool-looking tricks and having the patience and durable bodies needed to figure out these more difficult tricks. Today, you will find kids in the boys/girls I division (nine years and under) cranking off flips and doing advanced tricks that in the past weren't taught until much later. Learning has accelerated with the rising popularity of wakeboards and the crossover of skateboarders and snowboarders. Because of this evolution, we will pass over some of the other two-ski tricks and get things moving on one trick ski.

Skill 1: One-Ski Drills

Many skiers are instantly more comfortable on one trick ski or a wakeboard than on two trick skis. Sometimes this is because they have a strong slalom background, or surfing, skateboarding, or snowboarding experience. Either way, the key to success on one trick ski or a wakeboard is the same as on two skis—learning to ride and control the ski from different positions and angles. With some small adaptations, you perform the basic one-ski tricks just as you do the two-ski versions. We will cover those changes briefly and venture into toe tricks and a few more complicated tricks that will build your talent foundation before we start cranking off flips and body overs.

Begin with the same drills you did on two skis—edging through and popping off the wakes, pulling in, and advancing on the boat. Add the following drills to become more agile on your single trick ski.

Cutting and Edging on One Foot.   If you are riding a trick ski, take your foot out of the rear toe loop and aggressively cut and edge across the wakes. This will teach you balance, edge control, and how to position yourself over the ski for line and toe tricks. The key to this drill is learning to angulate by dropping your hip away from the handle as you set your edge, as illustrated in figure 6.11. You can perform the same drill on a wakeboard with both feet in the bindings. The key is learning to drop your hip away from the rope, toward the wake, to better angulate through the wakes.

Cutting and Edging Using the Toe Strap.   Do the same thing with your foot in the toe strap. Putting your foot in the toe strap for the first time can be a bit nerve racking, so practice on land just as you do with any new trick. Pull the handle in and grab the rope in front of the toe strap. Take your back foot out of the binding and slide it into the toe strap. Now slowly let the slack rope out with your hand and foot. You must stay on your toes and keep your knees bent during the entire process, as demonstrated in figure 6.12.

Unless you have a trick release, do not even try toe tricks. It's not worth blowing out a knee or tearing a hamstring. You can buy releases for all types of boats. A split pin release is shown in figure 6.13.

Figure 6.11   **Cutting and edging across the wakes with your foot out of the rear toe loop on a slalom trick will teach you balance and edge control.**

Figure 6.12 After you can cut and edge with your foot out of the rear toe loop, practice the same thing with your foot in the toe strap.

Figure 6.13 Split pin trick release.

Use the release for toe, line, body over, and any wrapped tricks. Selecting a dependable pin person is important. Choose someone who will not be distracted or lose focus on you. You want your pin person to err always on the side of caution rather than cost you a season with a preventable injury.

Skill 2: Basic One-Ski and Wakeboard Tricks

The basic one-ski tricks are front to back, back to front, 360, and the reverse and wake versions (see figure 6.14) of these tricks.

These tricks are more similar to the two-ski version than they are different. The concept is the same. Start in good body position and advance on the boat with a strong, even pull on the handle to the waist. Initiate the turn with the hips and shoulders, release with the hand, and reach for the handle. For the 360, you pass the handle and continue the rotation forward. Keep your eyes focused on the horizon and the handle close to the body. It is essential to maintain proper body position through the trick so you do not fall off the axis of rotation. It is smart to become comfortable riding the single ski backward and learning to edge the ski across the wakes. Be patient. Learn the reverses after you learn the basic trick. The box below gives the sequence in which you should learn hand tricks.

SEQUENCING FOR LEARNING HAND TRICKS

Description (code)

Side slide (S)
Reverse side slide (RS)
Front to back (B)
Back to front (F)
Reverse front to back (RB)
Reverse back to front (RF)
360 degree front to front (O)
Reverse 360 front to front (RO)
Wake back (WB)
Wake front (WF)
Reverse wake back (RWB)
Reverse wake front (RWF)
Wake 360 wrapped (WO)
Reverse wake 360 wrapped (RWO)
Wake 360 hand to hand (WO)

Reverse wake 360 hand to hand (RWO)
Surface wrap back (B)
Reverse surface wrap back (RSWB)
360 back to back (OB)
Reverse 360 back to back (ROB)
Wake 360 back to back (WOB)
Reverse wake 360 back to back (RWOB)
Wake 540 front (wrap in & hand to hand) (W5F)
Reverse wake 540 front (RW5F)
Wake 540 back (from wrap & hand to hand) (W5B)
Reverse wake 540 back (RW5B)

Figure 6.14   Wake back.

Performing these tricks on a wakeboard requires that you make a small hop to break the fin from the water before you make the rotation to the back position. Practice by jumping up and down on the board as if you were hopping the wakes. Once you get the hop down, initiate the rotation with your hips and shoulders. The difference is that you will not go all the way to the back position on a wakeboard. You will simply switch your stance, having the opposite foot toward the boat. This is known as riding fakie, shown in figure 6.15.

Skill 3: Setup Tricks

Setup tricks, such as the half wrap and reverse half wrap, are used to make advanced tricks easier and basic versions of some tricks (like the back to back) quicker. They are not that difficult to turn but can be hard to hold because of the turning of the body and the pull from the boat. They are much easier on a wakeboard because of the fins, so you may choose to try them on a wakeboard first. Taking the time to master these tricks opens you up to back to backs, 540s, and 720s.

Figure 6.15   Riding fakie.

Half Wrap.   To learn the basic half wrap, begin in basic skiing position. This is similar to switching to riding fakie. Turn the ski or board in the direction of your front foot and keep both hands on the handle. Force the ski to the back position using the hips, knees, and feet. As you can see in figure 6.16, the handle remains close to the body, with the knees and ankles well bent and back and shoulders straight and level with the water. Try to keep your upper body facing forward. The pull should be from the center of your body. This may require you to hold the handle behind your hip or lower back. If you are having trouble holding the position, try it outside the wake and use the wake to hold the ski in the backward position (left side for right foot forward). It is also helpful to put more weight on the back foot by flexing your knees to control the edge and get the ski to track better. If you are still having difficulty holding the half-wrap position, try turning more slowly so that you almost break the trick into a side slide with an extra 90 degrees of rotation. This will help you develop handle control during the trick.

Figure 6.16   Half wrap.

Reverse Half Wrap.   The reverse half wrap is done the same way but in the opposite direction. Most skiers find this trick more difficult to hold than the basic trick. It requires an awkward position and will take time to master, but the payoff is high-point tricks. Use the wake to help hold the position, right side for right foot forward. Concentrate on the handle. Keep it in tight to your body and find a position that allows you to hold the handle low with the pressure on the hand closest to the boat.

Back to Back.   Once you've mastered the half wrap and reverse half wrap, learning both surface and wake back to backs will be quick and easy. Simply do a half wrap, give a slight pull as you come forward, and continue the rotation to the reverse half wrap. By keeping both hands on the handle, the ski will rotate the full 360, while the body will turn much less. Less body movement coupled with a strong starting position means quick, easy tricks that you can perform without having to pass the handle. Some skiers find the back to backs easier if they start from the reverse half wrap position, turn to the half wrap, and then turn back to the reverse. By taking time to learn to edge in the half-wrapped positions, the wake back to back and reverse will be a breeze to learn.

Skill 4: Toe Turns

The basic toe turns are the toe back, toe front, toe wake back, and toe wake front. Always use a trick release and a competent pin person when learning these tricks.

Before trying these tricks you must become comfortable riding your ski with your foot in the toe strap. The secret, as in all forms of skiing, is body position. Focus on keeping your ski leg bent at the knee and ankle and your weight over the center of the ski on the ball of your foot. Figure 6.17 reveals the body position for toe tricks. Keep the rope leg bent and close to the ski leg; one to two feet away is perfect. Keep the back and shoulders straight and use the arms for balance. You should also learn to pull in and let out the rope with the toe strap, similar to the drill you did when learning the two-ski back. Now it is time to turn more heads by skiing backward with no hands. The box on page 133 shows the sequence in which you should learn toe tricks.

Toe Back.   Begin by pulling in on the rope to advance on the boat. With the line slightly loose, rotate your ski and body in a smooth, definite motion to the back position. As always, keep your eyes on the horizon and shoulders up. Focus on keeping the rope knee up. Maintain your rotational axis by keeping your weight centered over the ski during the turn and into the back position. The most common errors,

Figure 6.17 Body position for toe tricks: ski leg bent at the knee and ankle, and your weight over the center of the ski on the ball of your foot.

SEQUENCING FOR LEARNING TOE TRICKS

Description (code)

Toe back (TB)
Toe front (TF)
Toe wake front (TWF)
Toe wake back (TWB)
Toe side slide (TS)
Wrapped toe side slide (WTS)
Toe 360 front to front (TO)
Toe wake 360 (TWO)
Reverse toe back (RTB)
Reverse toe front (RTF)

Toe 360 wrap in from the back
   (stop in the back) (TO)
Toe 360 back to back (TOB)
Toe 540 back (T5B)
Toe 540 front (T5F)
Toe 720 front (T7F)
Toe wake 360 back (TWOB)
Reverse toe wake 360 back to back
   (RTWOB)
Toe steps (advanced)

which often occur together, are dropping the head during the turn and letting the rope away from the body. You can resolve these errors by making a strong, smooth pull on the rope and keeping the rope-leg knee near the ski-leg knee. Once you get to the back position, concentrate on maintaining correct position and becoming comfortable riding the ski. Play around. Learn the feel of shifting your weight and edging by dropping your hip toward the wake. Notice how the ski feels when skiing backward with your foot on the rope. Practice letting the handle out and pulling it back in. Don't forget to give a wave to all those jealous onlookers as you cruise down the lake.

Toe Front. The toe front causes trouble for some skiers, but once you understand the shift in weight and body position that occurs during the turn, you can master it easily. Start in a low position with your weight on your toes and make a firm pull in with the rope leg. Lead the turn with the hips and shoulders and keep the ski leg flexed. Some skiers have trouble here. The common fall is to rock your weight back onto the heel as you turn. Think about keeping your weight forward and on your toes as you rotate. Your shoulders need to remain level with the water and can come forward slightly as you come forward.

Toe Wake Back and Toe Wake Front. The toe wake back and toe wake front are both easy tricks to do once you get comfortable with the surface tricks. Prepare for these tricks by learning to edge up and through the wakes in both the forward and backward positions. As with all wake tricks it is usually easier to slide the tricks when first learning them. Start in a low position on your ski by flexing your knees and ankles, and hold an edge to the top of the wake. Push off the wake as you pull on the rope and initiate the turn as if you are doing a toe back, as demonstrated in figure 6.18. To prevent the ski from skipping out from under you as you land, keep your ski leg soft and flexed and the rope leg in close to the ski knee. The key to this trick is learning the correct pull before the turn and edging to the top of the wake before starting the turn.

Many skiers learn the toe wake front faster than the surface toe front because the wake helps with the forward weight shift that is critical for mastering this trick. From the toe back position outside the wake, set a firm edge toward the wake to keep tension on the rope. At the crest of the wake push off the wake with the ski leg to get lift. Pull in on the rope leg to begin your rotation to the front. As with the surface trick, the most troublesome aspect of the toe wake front is learning to stay over the center of the ski and maintaining your axis during the turn. To achieve this, keep the rope tight and close to the body. It sometimes helps to reach forward as you come forward to avoid the out-the-back fall.

Figure 6.18   Toe wake back and toe wake front.   *(continued)*

Figure 6.18   *(continued)*

DIFFICULT TRICKS MADE EASY

The tricks that really fire up the crowd and get the screams from the fans are the big air tricks. Flips, body overs, and ralleys are all amazing to watch, but be prepared to take a few hard falls when learning them. Sticking to the tips given above will save you some pain, but to land these awe-inspiring tricks you have to be willing to go for it. By becoming proficient at the drills described in this chapter, you will have the solid fundamentals needed to land these big-point tricks.

Flip

Begin from a few feet outside the wake on the side of your front foot, on the right side of the wake for right foot forward and vice versa for left. Allow your arms to relax and straighten out. Shift your weight over your front foot before you make your turn toward the wake and set your edge.

Make a slow, controlled, progressive turn and set your edge by dropping your hip into the wake. Maintain your edge by progressively cutting harder all the way through the top of the wake, keeping your weight over your front foot (figure 6.19a, b). As you pass through the top of the wake, push the tip of your ski or board backward, away from the boat (figure 6.19c).

As the ski passes up and over your head, allow the rope to pull you and your ski around to the forward position (figure 6.19d). Spot your landing by looking for the boat. Soften your knees for impact (figure 6.19e). Allow the ski to slide down the wake in the direction from which you began your cut (figure 6.19f).

Ski Line Back

Begin the body over, as the ski line tricks are known, in a relaxed comfortable position with your arms out slightly and your weight over your

TRICK TRAINING TIPS

As the tricks become more difficult, you will encounter more falls and frustrations. Here are a few tips that will keep you positive and help you maintain steady progress.

1. To prevent yourself from getting into a rut or becoming too frustrated, make no more than five attempts on a new trick.
2. Learn tricks in an order that is natural for you, but don't make the mistake of avoiding the reverses.
3. Take time to become proficient at the drills and preps we discussed. Doing so will allow you to have quick successes rather than becoming stuck on one trick because you have not perfected the fundamentals.
4. Do whatever you need to do to stand up on the trick. Never just throw the handle because you are out of position. Hold on and fight your way to success.
5. Keep your sets to 15 or 20 minutes. Even though tricking and boarding takes less strength than slalom, fatigue sets in and you lose some of your pull and balance. The concentration essential to make progress in tricking usually wanes after a time.
6. Break down every trick to its basics and learn it that way. A 540 front to back is simply a 360, which you can do easily, followed by a half wrap, which you can do. Perform the trick this way with a pause. Then slowly shorten the pause and continue the rotation.

a

b

c

d

Figure 6.19   Flip. *(continued)*

e   f

Figure 6.19   *(continued)*

front foot. Take a slow, smooth edge up the wake as you begin a strong pull on the rope toward the hip that is closest to the wake (figure 6.20a). A key at this stage of the trick is to keep your shoulders up and even with the water's surface, just as they are when you start the trick.

Continue to pull the handle to the side of your hip all the way through the top of the wake. You should have both hands in the handle as long as possible to get a full advance on the rope (figure 6.20b).

Finish the pull to your hip as you edge through the top of the wake. Let go of the handle with your outside arm and pull your knees up to your chest (figure 6.20c). At this point, your long, slow, progressive pull to your hip has advanced you far enough into the boat that you should easily pass over the line without jumping or throwing your shoulders off axis.

Once you pass over the rope, begin to put your legs down, keeping your knees soft to absorb the impact of landing (figure 6.20d). The handle needs to be as close to your hip as possible. Remember to keep your head and eyes up and focused on the horizon.

a

b

c

d

Figure 6.20   Ski line back.

Air Ralley

This trick has quickly separated the riders from the fliers in the wakeboard world. Begin by pulling out wide on your back side (left side of the boat for right foot forward and right side of the boat for left foot forward), make a smooth progressive turn, and set a hard edge as shown in figure 6.21a. Maintain the edge through the wake and out away from the boat.

At first just jump over the wakes and learn to control the board and edge. As you begin to take a more aggressive edge, let the handle out away from your body and let the board travel from under you as shown in figures 6.21b and c. Move the board out in small increments until you can fully extend it above your head. You should feel a stretch of your abdominal muscles as the board travels from under you.

DEVELOPING A TRICK RUN

The first step to developing a trick run is to get a pen and paper and make four columns. Write 100 percent, 80 percent, 50 percent, and New as headings for the columns, and enter the tricks you can do that fit into each category. List in the New column tricks you are working on or want to learn. The real secret to this step is being honest with yourself. Do not overestimate your abilities by placing tricks in 80 percent list that you make only 50 percent of the time. This list forms the foundation of your trick run. How you use this list will determine your success.

The next step is to write down the point value of each trick on your list. (Point values and descriptions of every trick and move are listed in chapter 8.) Now, write down last year's trick run and corresponding point value for each trick. It is possible that you can gain the points you need to reach your target by simply replacing an easy trick with a higher value trick. An example would be to change a WBB, R, WF, WB sequence to WBB, R, W5F, WB. Changing one trick (doing a W5F instead of a WF) would gain you 230 points toward your goal with no change in sequence or run design. A second strategy is to replace low-point tricks with newly mastered high-point tricks. If you learn a flip and use it to replace a time-consuming sequence such as WB, WF, R, R, you gain 180 points and a second or two that you can use for another trick and more points. You should develop a run that is a few hundred points over your target to provide a safety margin in competition. Make your run worth 3,200 to attain a score of 3,000. Here are a few pointers for putting your run together:

a

b

c

d

Figure 6.21   Air ralley.

1   Always use a trick from your 100 percent list as your opening trick. You must be comfortable and confident in your first trick. You have to stand up to score a personal best.
2. Position the 80 percent tricks in spots that allow you to recover before attempting another difficult trick. Do this by inserting an easy 100 percent trick between more difficult tricks. For example, put a BB between an RWBB and W5F. This addition allows you to gather yourself if a problem occurs in the first trick, yet still gains you points.
3. Try to link your sequences with as few positioning tricks as possible.
4. Use your time intelligently. You have only 20 seconds in a run, enough time for about 14 tricks. Don't try to cram an extra 4 tricks into your run to reach your goal. You are unlikely to reach it if you rush and have credit pulled or fall.
5. Use the 50 percent tricks as reward tricks. Once you stand up your run, celebrate by landing a hard trick. Take your time, relax (you can because you have not included these tricks into your 3,000), and nail the trick. View these tricks as a bonus. Soon they will become 80 percent or 100 percent tricks.
6. Use drills and preps to speed up the learning of new tricks. The lifeblood of every tricker, new tricks can transform a 3,000-point run into a 5,000-point run.

Now that you have done the math and filled out your "dream sheet," it's time to put it to the test on the water. The quickest way to learn a new run is to break it into sections or sequences—five or six tricks that go together. Sequences like B, BB, R, WBB, R, W5F and TO, TB, TF, TS fit together and promote speed and consistency. Practice these sequences slowly and with control until they become comfortable and flow together. Speed is not a concern at this stage. Focus on being smooth and consistent; speed will come once you develop confidence and solid fundamentals.

CHAPTER 7

JUMP SKIING

If you are an adrenaline junkie, if you are a thrill seeker, if you list sky diving, bungee jumping, or hang gliding as things you want to do or have done, then water ski jumping is a rush you need to experience. Professional jumpers travel farther over a flat surface than athletes in any other sport, even Evil Knievel. In simple terms, they fly!

Professional jumping has its spills, chills, and bone-rattling crashes, but crashes are actually rare and are always the fault of jumpers extending their limits a little too far. The body busters you see on television and on the Pro Tour do one thing—scare people out of their skin and instill a fear of jumping. Jumping does have its risks, but when learned properly it is an extremely safe event. All skiers should at least attempt several rides over the miniramp, if for no other reason than to brag to their friends that they have conquered the "enchanted slanted." My bet is that anyone who tries jumping will become an instant adrenaline junkie and start jumping every time they have a chance. The feeling of floating in the air is addictive. You will be wanting more.

JUMPING FUNDAMENTALS

To eliminate the natural fear associated with your first time over the ramp, U.S. team coach Jay Bennett has developed a new jump learning system. The miniramp instructional program has been 100 percent successful in teaching students to jump. The program is safer than the traditional "off the side of the ramp" method used at some ski schools, and uses a skills progression that is proven to work. The objective of this section is first to learn to ride and control the jump skis and then build confidence and eliminate fear by using the miniramp. Once we get the fundamentals down, we will gradually raise the ramp to competition height.

Skill 1: Body Position

If you are like most of us, as soon as you could get up on two skis you started trying to slalom. Because of this, few people ever really become comfortable on two skis, much less jump skis, which are wider, longer, and a little more difficult to control than combo pairs. To get started, let's review basic body position. Keep head up, elbows in, ankles and knees bent, and feet shoulder-width apart. Hold the handle with the left-hand palm up and right-hand palm down as shown in figure 7.1. Have your shoulders straight and chest forward to keep your weight on your toes. Take the time to get your position set on land before going to the water. Once on the water get in correct position and start playing around on the skis.

Spend several ski sets riding your skis to get your body position correct and learn to control your skis. If you are a snow skier, it will be easy. You ride jump skis just as you ride snow skis. Riding your skis and jumping

Figure 7.1   Remember to practice basic body position on land before taking it to the water.

the wakes will teach you the balance and edge control that will be necessary to make your first jump. Try running the slalom course at slow speed, about 15 mph, on jump skis. This drill is great for beginners just learning to ride jumpers. Jump skis glide more than combo skis and turn differently, so body position is crucial. Become accustomed to the feel of jump skis and start trying to jump the wakes by pushing with your lower body while keeping your skis together. Do not use your shoulders or upper body as you would in sports like basketball. As you land, absorb the landing with your knees as you would if you jumped off a chair. Gradually build confidence until you are able to ride the skis with good body position and edge control.

Skill 2: Overcoming the Wall

You will want to eliminate two common problems before you ever go over the ramp. The first problem is the wall. The first time you approach it, the ramp will look like a wall, and you will have a tendency to lean back onto your heels. This position will cause the skis to slide out in front of you when you hit the ramp, and the handle will come toward your chest or chin. A great drill to avoid this error is to try running up a hill while leaning back as far as you can. You can't do it. You end up running up the hill with your shoulders forward. This is the same way you should go over the ramp, as seen in figure 7.2.

Figure 7.2 To keep your skis from sliding out in front of you the first time over the jump, keep your shoulders forward.

Skill 3: The Arc Method

The second problem is lining up to the ramp. The secret to a successful first jump is learning to keep your skis flat with no edge as you ride over the miniramp. You must line up to the jump with equal weight on both feet and the skis flat, as shown in figure 7.3. Fighting the pull of the boat will lead to unequal weight distribution and cause the skis to slip out to the side with too much weight. To prevent this problem from occurring, learn the arc method. This method requires some depth perception, timing, and practice, but it is the safest, quickest, and most successful way to learn to jump.

The setup shown in figure 7.4 is how you prevent needless falls, save time, and increase your chances of riding out your first jump. You don't want to learn this at the jump, so we simulate a jump with buoys from a slalom course.

Run the boat just inside the skier buoys as shown. Pick out two gate buoys and pull out to the side of the boat approximately 10 feet outside of the gate buoys. Then stop pulling and put the skis on a flat edge. (You can tell when the skis are on a flat edge if there is equal spray coming from both sides.) Let the boat pull you back through the two buoys and into the wakes. Your path of travel will resemble an arc,

Figure 7.3 Line up to the jump with your skis flat and with equal weight on both feet.

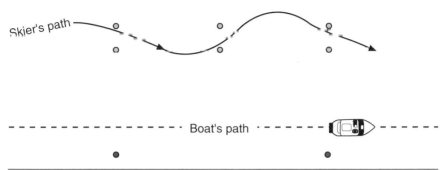

Figure 7.4   Practice the arc method using slalom course buoys.

accounting for the name of the drill. As you are going through the buoys, imagine that you are going over the ramp. Remember, think about holding perfect body position and keeping the skis flat as you drift in through the buoys. Do this drill until you have it down. It is worth the time for the added confidence it will give you. A little trick to check whether you are in correct position is to hook the rope to the trick release and have someone pin you without warning as the boat pulls you back to the wakes. You will hardly notice you have been pinned if you are in correct body position. You will simply glide to a stop and sink into the water. If your weight is back or if you are on edge, you will take a nice spill on your butt.

GOING OVER THE RAMP

Before you attempt to go over the five-foot ramp, you should become comfortable jumping on the miniramp. The miniramp was invented in response to ski school students' fear of the regular ramp. A full ramp is an imposing slanted wall of steel, wood, and fiberglass that can be intimidating to first timers. You wouldn't ask beginning snow skiers to ski down a black diamond slope for their first run. You would send them down the bunny slope first because they would be less fearful and have more confidence that they could make it. The same is true for the miniramp. It is much smaller—half the height—and visually less imposing. This means more confidence and a higher success rate. So let's go over!

Skill 1: Going Over the Miniramp

Having mastered correct body position and the optimal approach, you approach the moment of truth. Relax; you are prepared and will do fine. Take a few deep breaths. Gather your gear, helmet, jump suit, gloves, and jump skis. Run the boat about 25 feet outside the ramp on the path shown in figure 7.5. Pull out to the left of the jump and arc over the ramp as you see in figure 7.6. It's that easy!

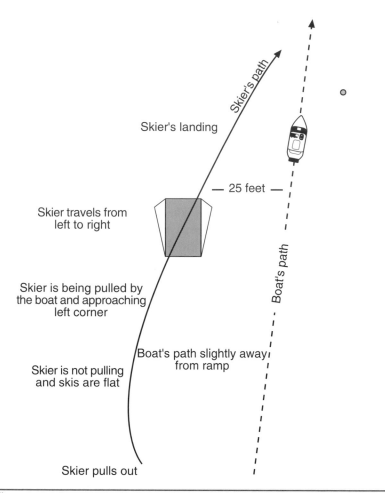

Figure 7.5   Boat and skier paths for going over the miniramp.

Here are a few pointers:

- Use correct body position (knees and ankles bent, etc.).
- Look over the top of the jump or at the tops of trees.
- Keep your skis flat.
- Freeze—don't let the boat pull you out of position.

On the landing you will have a tendency to lean back, especially if you look down and see the water. Try to act as if you are jumping off a chair—land on the balls of your feet, not your bum. Here are some tips for landing:

- Keep your upper body still and quiet, with little or no motion.
- Keep the handle down near your hips.

Figure 7.6   Arcing over the miniramp.

- Keep your head up looking at the tree tops.
- Keep your elbows at your side.
- Keep your knees over your feet.
- Have the driver turn back into the ramp slightly as you come off the ramp. This will give you a straighter pull and easier landing.

I recommend that you use a trick release while learning to jump. If you fall into the rope, a simple tug on the string will prevent injury. More than 90 percent of students who use the miniramp system ride out their first jump. I have never seen it fail to teach a student to jump. It is important to build on success and take the time to perfect each stage. Spend several sets practicing and perfecting your skills on the miniramp before proceeding. Perfect your arc and body position before taking the next step. The result with this system is always the same—you become addicted, a jumpaholic, wanting your next fix over the ramp.

Skill 2: Moving Up to the Full Ramp

The next challenge for the newly christened jumper is moving up to the full-size ramp. This is usually an easy transition because you are confident and have mastered the correct technique by going over the miniramp 10 or 20 times. We further lessen the impact of this transition by setting the ramp height at 3 ½ to 4 feet rather than the 5-foot regulation height. From that point on nearly everything is identical to jumping on the miniramp. The only two differences are the amount of time you will be on the ramp's surface and the height from which you will land. To handle the increased time on the ramp, you simply need to hold your body position longer. The miniramp is slightly shorter than a full ramp. The impact on touching down will be greater, so again, you must hold correct body position and execute a proper arc over the ramp. The driver should follow the same path and speed used on the miniramp. Jump at the lower height for a few sets until you are confident in your body position and landings.

The next progression is to move the ramp up to the full five-foot height. Your body position and proper arc are again the keys to success. The boat driver will run the same pattern, but at a slightly faster speed— 2 mph faster—to keep your tips from dropping and to prevent falls on the ramp. You will do the same setup but pull out to a wider position for your arc. Since you are wider, you will need to pull out sooner. Keep your skis flat, head up, and ankles bent. Ski over the ramp and stick a perfect landing. Have a camera and photographer in the boat to catch this moment on film. You will be excited, to say the least, and the falls, if you have them, are always worth a laugh or two.

TROUBLESHOOTING BEGINNING JUMPS

FALL: Skis sliding out on the ramp.

Error: You are not on flat skis as you go over the ramp.
Solution: Make sure your skis are flat on the water. Use no edge approach.

FALL: Your ride over is fine, but you fall back onto your butt when you hit the water.

Error: Weight is on your heels or you pull the handle in to your chest.
Solution: Flex your knees and ankles to shift more weight to your toes, and press the handle down, keeping your elbows at your hips.

FALL: You fall forward on landing.

Error: Your shoulders are too far forward or your knees and ankles are not bent enough.
Solution: Straighten your back until your chest is up, but bend slightly at the waist to keep your weight on your toes. Lower your butt to the water by flexing your knees and ankles.

A few final words to new jumpers. The miniramp is the preferred method of learning how to jump. It is safer, gives you more confidence, and makes for a smoother transition to the full ramp. Unfortunately, many ski schools and sites are not willing to spend the money necessary to improve their instructional jumping program. The student pays the price by taking unnecessary falls and suffering from the intimidation of the large ramp. If this is your situation, then you can do one of two things: Find a ski school with a miniramp or try skiing over the side of the ramp. The process for skiing over the side of the ramp is similar to skiing the miniramp. You pull out, flatten your skis, and do an arc over the corner of the ramp as shown in figures 7.7 and 7.8.

The boat must travel a different pattern, and coming off the ramp is slightly more difficult because the edge of the ramp is at different heights. From there, the learning progression is identical to jumping on the miniramp. Your next step is to put the ramp into its lowest height and go over the top. Then move it up to the five-foot height. Either way, body position and proper arc are crucial for success.

Figure 7.7   Skiing over the side of the ramp.

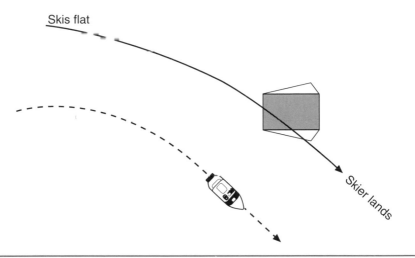

Skis flat

Skier lands

Figure 7.8   Boat and skier paths for skiing over the side of the ramp.

JUMP DRILLS

Now that you have successfully conquered the "big red monster" and are a certified jumpaholic, you want to jump farther. You crave the feeling of weightlessness as you fly through the air; you hunger for more hang time. If distance is your quest, speed and lift will get you there. In this section we will master the first element of the distance-jumping equation—speed. Not just any speed, but controlled speed. And don't fret; we will also begin working on the lift side of the equation.

The concept of controlled speed begins with the fundamental skill of edge control. To go long distances in jumping, you must be able to generate speed. With more speed the danger factor increases, as does fear. How do you learn to manage danger and fear? By being in control of their cause, speed. How do you control speed? With the edges of your skis. Until now, you have been jumping on flat skis, with no edge. Now it is time to learn how to control your edges and really ride those jump skis. Here are two drills to teach you how to generate controlled speed through edge control.

Drill 1: No-Jump Jumping

Before you learned to jump we had you become comfortable riding the jump skis. You may have even tried the slalom course drill. If you have not, try it now. Start off at the #1 ball and try to run the course on your jump skis. Keep the boat speed slow, at 15 mph, and make a pass. This is a good beginner's drill, but now that you are jumping, you need to learn how to hold your edge through the ramp. The slalom course is no longer useful. Instead, we simulate exactly what we are doing—jumping.

The skier pattern for advanced jumping is called a double cut. The first phase of the no-jump drill is simulating the double-cut pattern without going over the ramp (we will discuss the second phase in the advanced section). Ski the pattern away from the jump course so the ramp is nowhere near. Alternatively, ski the jump course but start the pattern later so when you turn toward the ramp you are well past it, as shown in figure 7.9. Pro jumpers do this drill endlessly. It is great for conditioning in the preseason and teaches you control of the skis without your having to worry about timing or the ramp. The first few times you attempt this drill you will most likely be cutting on both skis. You

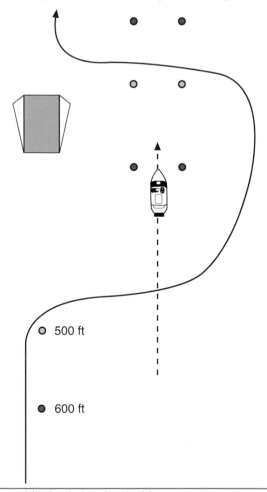

Figure 7.9   No-jump drill simulating the double-cut pattern.

should emphasize cutting on the ski closest to the boat as you cross the wakes. Your goal is to have 90 percent of your weight on that ski as you cut through the wakes.

During a double cut, body position is crucial as always. The upper body should remain very still. Most of the movement should occur in the ankles and knees as you push away from the boat on your right ski, edging through the wakes. Do this by dropping your hip away from the boat or angulating.

To get the feeling of dropping your hip, stand one to two feet from a wall or tree and get into basic ride-over position with your side facing the wall or tree. Now act as if you are edging across the wakes. You should drop your hip so both the hip and your shoulder are touching the wall or tree as seen in figure 7.10. The shoulders must remain up and square to the skis, while the arms are low with the elbows to the sides and the hands together.

If you are having trouble holding this position, lower the boat speed until you can maintain perfect position while cutting through the wakes and up the side of the boat. Try 25 mph to start. Pro jumpers work constantly on dropping the hip and maintaining position across the course. It is a good idea for you to perfect this skill now.

Figure 7.10   Practice on land to get the feeling of dropping your hip.

Drill 2: The Crane

The crane is similar to the no-jump drill, but much more difficult. You will follow the same pattern, but when you do the crane you will lift the outside ski (the one closest to the boat as you pull out). Slow the boat to a comfortable speed, 20 to 25 mph, and pull out to the side. Make a slow, smooth turn and lift the inside ski, closest to the wake, one foot off the water as you set your edge. Concentrate on staying low in your ski by dropping your hip and bending your ankles and knees as seen in figure 7.11. Keep the handle down and elbows in. Keep pulling through both wakes and drop your hip even more as you come off the second wake. Maintain the crane until you are up on the side of the boat. Put the ski down, slow down, and make another smooth turn back through the wake on the opposite ski.

This drill is the best drill I have seen for teaching someone how to control their jump skis and drop the hip for correct body position. As stated earlier, you should have 90 percent of your weight on your edging ski as you cross the wakes. This ski is known as the working ski. The crane stresses the working ski by forcing you to put 100 percent of your weight on it and still maintain perfect edging position.

Figure 7.11   The crane drill will teach you how to control your skis and drop your hip.

Drill 3: Wake Jumping

After doing the no-jump and the crane drills, you have a good feel for whatwe mean by controlled speed. You should continue to work on these drills until you master them. The next step to increasing your jump distance is learning how to get lift. When you learned to jump we taught you to freeze as you went over the ramp. This freezing was simply resisting the force of hitting the ramp. Now it is time to begin learning how to kick the ramp to get lift. The wake jump drill is a simple and easy way to learn the fundamentals of lift.

To begin, jump one wake by pushing with your lower body with your skis together. Do not use your shoulders or upper body as you would in sports like basketball. Edge up the wake and extend your knees and ankles while keeping your upper body still and handle in as seen in figure 7.12. Push straight up as you would on land; in fact, try it on land before taking it to the water. Now start from a wider position on the boat, take a harder edge, and carry more speed into the wakes. Edge up the wake and kick it. Keep doing this until you can clear both wakes in one jump.

Figure 7.12   Jumping the wake will help you learn how to get lift.

Once you can clear the wakes, do an arc over the ramp and try kicking it. Now you are ready for the next stage in learning how to increase your jumping distance—edging through the ramp.

EDGING THROUGH THE RAMP

Jumping has evolved from the days when skiers were taught to cut across the wakes, flatten out before the jump, and kick it. Today, through the use of computerized training and biomechanical analysis, we teach jumpers to edge through the ramp. This accomplishes the two things that create more distance: speed and lift. You will maintain the speed you have been working so hard to generate by holding your direction across the course and over the ramp. When you hold your edge across to the base of the ramp, you get more lift because stronger resistance is created on the ramp and the boat gives you a stronger pull off the ramp and through the air.

Until now, you have been either riding your skis to improve control and learn body position or arcing over the ramp on flat skis. Now it is time to put the two elements together and learn how to edge into the ramp. As we described earlier, edging involves pushing forward with the knees and the ankles, away from the rope's pull on the edges of the skis, especially the right ski. You must also drop the hip by angulating and pushing with the right knee to the left, away from the boat's direction. This position will accentuate the edge and create a stronger body position. This action is very similar to edging on snow skis. In addition, you must lead with the right ski into the ramp because it is doing most of the work and has more force upon it. This dropping of the hip and flexing of the knees and ankles, shown in figure 7.13, lowers your body's center of balance. You are now in a sitting position with the thighs at a right angle to the lower leg. As stated earlier, you should strive to maximize the edging, placing 90 percent of your weight on the right ski.

The upper body position is exactly the same as it was when you learned to ride over the ramp for the first time. The shoulders and head are square to the skis, and the arms are low. The difference is the direction of the pull. When you edge across the course, you must concentrate on edging to the left by pushing the right hand toward the left hip. This action will keep the shoulders aligned with the skis and counteract the boat's pull away from your body. Focus your eyes either on the top right corner of the ramp or into the horizon over that corner. The natural tendency is to look to the bottom left corner. This is a habit to avoid at all costs, so break it now.

Before getting into learning the techniques that allow you to edge through the ramp, let me first address an issue that confused me until it

Figure 7.13   Dropping your hip and flexing your knees and ankles lowers your body's center of balance as you edge into the ramp.

was properly explained and demonstrated. We have stressed keeping your skis flat on the ramp as you go over so the skis don't slide out. Now we are trying to get you to edge your skis through the ramp. How do you do that and not bust your bum? Jim Grew gives a simple explanation in the *AWSA Level III Coaches Manual:* "The skis are on edge coming into the ramp and the skier is going from right to left. The angle of the skis themselves will match the angle of the ramp." That may or may not answer the question, but it works and it is much safer and more controllable than trying to ride flat skis while carrying speed into the ramp. Simply stated, the pull of the boat as the skier edges across the course and into the ramp keeps the skis in proper position as you edge through the ramp. If you don't have confidence in this concept, watch the pros to get a feel for what we mean.

Skill 1: The Single-Wake Cut

This is where jumping and the jump put on a new face, and the real fun begins. You see the ramp from a new angle, one that makes you question if you can edge over it without skiing over the side curtain. Confidence is critical. Above all else, remember that jumping is a smart skier's event, not a crazy skier's challenge. If you dare challenge it without confidence and savvy, the ramp will, as Jay Bennett says with his south Louisiana twang, "eat your lunch." But have no fear if you have done the drills and taken the time to learn how to ride your jump skis. If you have been smart and are prepared, you have every reason to be confident, even cocky, about improving your distances because you have built a foundation that will take you far.

From now on, the word to remember about your jumping career is "progressive." You must learn to start smoothly and slowly and build your speed as your edge gets progressively stronger all the way through the ramp. It sounds easier than it is. When you are on the water, things seem to move a little quicker, and you tend to rush a bit. Calm down, slow down, and stay progressive with your edge. Now let's hit the wedge!

Have the driver run the boat parallel to the ramp, splitting the right side of the ramp and the 15-meter buoy as shown in figure 7.14a. The

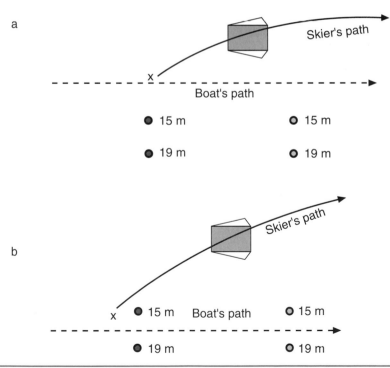

Figure 7.14   Boat path and skier path for learning the single-wake cut: (a) splitting the right side of the ramp and the 15-meter buoy and (b) splitting the 15-meter and 19-meter buoys.

ramp is set at five feet and the boat speed should be in the 24 mph range. As shown in figure 7.15a, position yourself just outside the left wake and assume basic body position, as you do in arcing.

Focus your eyes on the top left corner of the ramp and take a progressive edge up through the middle of the ramp, just as we described in the beginning of this section and as seen in figure 7.15b. It is just that simple. Your path should follow figure 7.14a to begin. The keys are to maintain a strong edge, correct body position, and good control throughout the edge and over the ramp.

You will feel the increased distance and begin to feel the float that is so addictive as you gain more confidence and take a harder edge and more speed into the ramp. After a few sets using this boat position, have the driver move the boat away from the ramp in two-foot increments until he or she is driving what is known as a split, splitting the 15-meter and 19-meter buoys as shown in figure 7.14b. This wider position will force you to maintain an edge longer and allow you to generate more speed into the ramp.

Here are a few quick tips and things to look for if you are having trouble landing or riding out your jumps. If you find that you are falling back on landing or the handle is coming up around your chin or chest in the air, one of two things is happening. You are flattening out your skis before you hit the ramp, causing you to pull up on the handle to keep it tight, or you are edging with your weight shifted back on your heels. In both cases, concentrate on keeping the handle down and elbows in to your sides as you press your right knee into the ramp.

The final phase of the single-wake cut is to increase the speed. Until now you have been learning to generate your own speed, controlling speed by edging your skis. Now it is time to adjust to the feeling of approaching at a faster boat speed. The difference is how you control your skis at faster speeds. The driver should increase speed in small increments (1 to 2 mph) and maintain the same boat pattern. You are still in charge of generating your speed, but now the boat will assist you by giving you greater resistance to push against through the ramp. The body position and cutting position remain the same. Most problems arise from lack of control, which causes loss of the edge into the ramp. If this happens, slow the boat speed 1 mph and try it again. The idea is to practice habits that are correct, not to form poor habits by practicing wrong things. Don't be too proud to slow the speed to maintain proper body position and gain controlled speed. By learning a progressive edge with controlled speed, you will have a longer jumping career in both distance and time.

a

b

c

d

Figure 7.15   The single-wake cut.   *(continued)*

e   f

Figure 7.15   *(continued)*

Skill 2: The Three-Quarter Cut

At this stage you should be jumping in the 50- to 80-foot range, but you know you can go farther. You can see the 100-foot buoy just in front of you when you land. Jumping has now gotten inside your head. It has become an obsession, a challenge, a rush like no other. Stay calm, stay smart, stick to the plan, and you will soon be jumping more than 100 feet. But before we go for it, let's get our heads on straight and prevent any needless crashes. You are at the most dangerous point in your jumping career; you have just enough talent and ability to hurt yourself if you push beyond your limits. Calm down and stay with our two basic concepts—speed control and progressive edging.

You don't want to rush into this phase of jumping. Be sure you have learned to edge progressively. Some top coaches keep their students jumping with a single cut for a full season or more to ensure that they can control their skis and speed. This may seem like a long time, but the skiers who learn to ride their skis end up improving more quickly. They have the safest jumps when they learn to jump from a wider position known as the three-quarter cut.

The three-quarter cut begins as nothing more than an extended version of the single cut you just learned. The difference is that you start from a slightly wider position, 10 feet outside the right wake. Keep the boat speed and path the same as you set it for your single cuts—28 to 30 mph, split. The same principles of progressive edging and controlled speed still apply, except now there is more timing involved. To help adjust to this new timing element without the worry of going over the ramp, do the no-jump jumping drill with one small addition—use buoys to simulate the ramp. If you have a jump course, and at this stage you should, use the second set of timing buoys to simulate the ramp. (If you don't have a jump course, set out two buoys to represent the ramp about 12 feet apart away from the ramp. Run the boat in a straight line about 50 feet outside the buoy closest to the boat.) Pull out 10 feet outside the wake, assume the correct body position, and focus on the left buoy, which represents the left top corner of the ramp. Don't worry about the wakes; let the boat slowly pull you over them as you set a soft edge. As you come off the second wake you should be near the same position you have been taking on your single cut. Drop your hip and edge up and through to the middle of the buoys. Try this until you are comfortable, confident, and in control of your body position, skis, and speed. Once you feel you are ready, take it to the ramp with confidence, concentrating on holding your edge as you drop your hip off the wake into the ramp. I doubt you will have any problem, but if you do, it will be one of the errors we discussed earlier.

Once you get solid at jumping from this wider position, move out a little farther—20 feet outside the wakes—and go through the same process. Now do the same thing from 30 feet. Figure 7.16 shows the skier's

EDGING THROUGH THE RAMP: A CHECKLIST

Just as any pilot goes through a checklist before and after a flight, you should do the same. Here are some things to think about before and after each jump.

1. Were you low in your skis with your weight on your toes before you turned to the ramp?
2. Were your eyes focused across the course and at the top left corner of the ramp?
3. Was your right ski slightly in front of the left as you set your edge across course?
4. Did you drop your hip and press your right knee into the ramp?
5. Was the handle low and were the elbows in to your hips?
6. Was 90 percent of your weight on the right ski?
7. Did you hold your direction across course and edge through the ramp?

Figure 7.16   The three-quarter cut.   *(continued)*

Figure 7.16   *(continued)*

path for the three-quarter cut. The farther you move out, the more speed you will carry into the base of the ramp, and the more critical body position and timing will become. You should be able to generate 80 to 90 percent of your maximum distance from a three-quarter cut, so you should spend a great deal of time mastering this technique. Take the time needed to become aware of your location in relation to the boat and ramp. Develop a sense of timing and stay safe and in control of your speed and position. If things aren't right, then pass!

Until now you have been running the boat between, or splitting, the jump course buoys (figure 7.17a). As you learn to take a stronger edge and ski across the course more, you will arrive at the ramp earlier. You

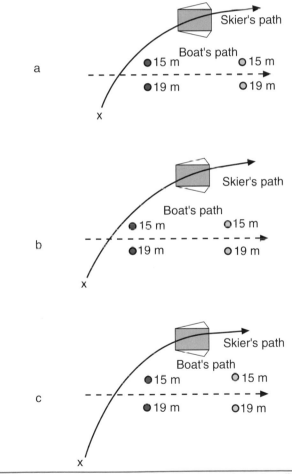

Figure 7.17 Skier and boat path for the three-quarter cut: splitting the jump course buoys (a). As you take a stronger edge across the course, begin to move the boat out toward the right-hand side of the course (b). Eventually you will find a spot from which you can comfortably take a full edge into the ramp (c).

can keep your turn at the same location and get back into a full cutting position by beginning to move the boat out wider toward the right-hand side of the course (figure 7.17b). Move it out in one- or two-foot increments until you find a spot that is comfortable for you to take a full, strong edge into the ramp as seen in figure 7.17c and figure 7.16.

Passing on a jump is a safety technique at this stage. Later, in the advanced section, we will use passing as a training technique, but at this stage in your career you should use it strictly for safety reasons. If you are early into the ramp, pass. If you are late into the ramp, pass. If you are on your heels, pass. If your skis are behind you, pass. If you don't have confidence, pass. Do not try to salvage a bad start or edge. By learning to pass you do two things: You stay safe, and you practice good habits of edging and turning slowly. You pass by letting go of the handle and skiing around the left side of the ramp. Avoid hitting any portion of the ramp. Hop over the corner if need be.

Passing is only a safety technique at this stage because passing on purpose teaches bad habits. The secret to good jumping is learning to edge through the ramp. When you pass you usually stop pulling just after the wakes, let go of the handle, and ski around the ramp. This is the exact op-posite of what you need to practice. Do not hesitate to pass if things are unsafe and you don't feel confident, but take the jump when things are good.

LONG JUMPS

If you have taken the time to master the skills and drills in the first two sections, you should now be jumping in the 100- to 130-foot range with a three-quarter cut on a 5-foot ramp at 30 to 32 mph. If you are not achieving this, go back and learn to jump at least those distances before using the advanced techniques we will now discuss. Believe me, it is worth it. As I write this I am a victim of ignoring my own advice. I skied in a jump tournament this weekend without taking time to refresh my jumping skills. Oh yes, I crashed, and I am in pain with sore and aching muscles from a trip out the back door. It hurts, trust me, so get this stuff down.

Our objective in this section is simple—increase distance by any means possible. This is where jumping can really get dangerous if you don't take the time to master the art of controlled speed. Proceed with caution and make sure you have mastered the fundamentals. Otherwise you will end up like me, with a neck that doesn't want to turn and a back so sore it hurts to lie down. It could be worse, but jumpers don't like to talk about that stuff!

Top jumpers are trying anything and everything to gain an extra foot or two on the competition. Speed suits, new ski designs, and different positions in the air are all having a great impact on the length and consistency of big jumps. Jumps of more than 200 feet have become commonplace on the Pro Tour, but fans never tire of watching the awesome speed, explosive lift, and heavenly float attained by today's best. What are the secrets of the world's best? It breaks down into five elements for increasing distance.

Extra Distance Gear

At this level of jumping, an arm sling, shown far left in figure 7.18, is essential. The purpose of the arm sling is to concentrate the pull of the boat at the center of the skier's body. This creates a stronger position and helps maintain body position through the wakes and in the air.

The sling is responsible for the kitelike lift that adds distance to the jump as the boat pulls the skier during the first half of the flight. You must still resist the pull from the boat with your back and arms to prevent being pulled out the front, but the sling makes it easier to hold on.

Speed and lift are the two primary forces that create big distance, but you must overcome a third factor, drag, to attain your full potential. Speed suits, shown third from left in figure 7.18, have been around since the 1980s. Today they seem to be standard issue rather than an experimental piece of equipment. By reducing drag through the wakes and in the air, the speed suit helps you overcome the one force that can slow you down. A great deal of experimentation is still going on with speed suits. Top skiers are trying new materials and shapes to achieve a more aerodynamic flow during flight.

Figure 7.18   **Extra distance gear.**

The biggest innovations in jumping today are happening with skis. The big dogs of jumping are going wild, experimenting with longer skis, over 85 inches, larger and wider tips, as large as 12 inches, different rocker patterns, and side cuts and tapers that radically change turning and edging characteristics of the skis. It seems to be paying off. Skiers are jumping 210 to 220 more frequently than ever.

Skill 1: The Double Cut

As we stated earlier, you should be able to achieve nearly all of your distance from a three-quarter cut. Where does the rest come from? The double cut. The purpose of the double cut is to position the skier out wider. From a wider position on the boat, the skier is able to create more angle across the wakes and generate more speed into the ramp. The skier and boat path are shown in figure 7.19.

The increased angle and speed equal greater distance. The trade-off is consistency. The wider you get on the boat, the more critical the timing of the turn and cut. This is where the cut and pass drill can be beneficial.

The purpose of this drill is to learn the timing of your turn and cut without worrying about the ramp. You should use this drill to see the new perspective of the ramp and boat and make any adjustments. To use this drill effectively, you must make a turn and cut as if you were actually going to hit the ramp, let go at the last possible second, and safely get around the ramp.

Two additional elements are essential for big jumps using the double cut. You must learn how to make the counter cut. The counter cut is different from the cut to the ramp. Its only purpose is to position you wider on the boat; thus a more leveraged position, similar to slalom, is required. The timing of the turn for the counter cut is assisted by the 500- and 600-foot buoys. You will pull out to the left side of the boat and use a snowplow position to control speed for the turn. Once you turn the skis, apply pressure to the left ski and pull through the wakes across the course and up to the side of the boat. When you have achieved your maximum width, you need to pull the handle up and across your body. This extra action gives you additional speed and advances you farther up on the boat. As you glide down the lake you prepare for the next phase of the double cut, the turn. The double-cut turn is different from the three-quarter cut turn. Since you are farther up on the side of the boat, you cannot make the same turn without getting slack in the rope or dropping back to a more narrow position. You must learn the S turn to solve this problem.

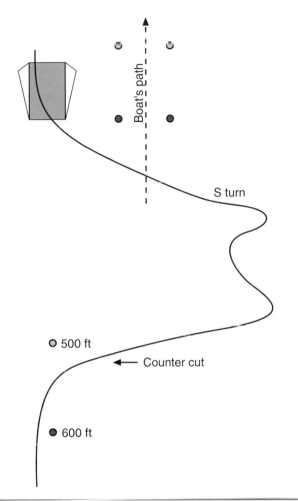

Figure 7.19   Skier and boat path for the double cut.

The key to the S turn is to make a slow rotation toward the ramp. This sounds easy, but when you are looking across the course and see the side curtain of the ramp, you have a tendency to rush everything. You can overcome this by cutting and passing, and learning a proper S turn. The S turn begins by letting your left arm extend out during the glide. As you glide, rotate the left hip away from the boat. This action edges you away from the ramp and keeps the rope tight. Now shift your weight to your right ski and make a slow rotation with the right hip back to the handle. This entire turn is shown in figure 7.20. Fix your eyes across course, not on the ramp; flex your knees; and keep the handle down and in near the body. Set your edge and hold your direction across the wakes as you have been doing with the three-quarter cut. It will be

Figure 7.20   The S turn.

slightly more difficult to hold the edge due to the increased angle. If you are having trouble, back up or spend more time practicing the drills you learned in the earlier sections.

Skill 2: The Safety Crush

You have just made a perfect turn and are right where you want to be. You set your edge and get a burst of speed that rockets you across the course and through the wakes. You look at the ramp as you cross the wakes and oh no—you feel yourself rock back on your heels. This sets off your safety alarm system. Abort. You know this is a bad position to be in, but it is too late to pass. What to do? If you hit the ramp it could mean a painful back or neck buster. The ramp is right there. You keep your head on straight and do a safety crush. Good decision!

The safety crush is one of the skills an advanced jumper must perfect if he or she is to have a lengthy career. If you find yourself in a less-than-desirable position and feel that trying to spring or resist the ramp will result in a crash, simply absorb the force of the ramp by allowing your legs to buckle up under your body. Like all skills, you must practice this technique until it becomes natural and controllable. The crush should be instinctive whenever you are in poor position approaching the ramp.

Skill 3: Raising the Ramp and Learning the Kick

Until now you have been jumping on a 5-foot ramp. You have mastered all the skills we have discussed. The next progression of learning is raising the ramp to 5 ½ feet to feel extra lift and distance. Conquer the bigger ramp with the same methods you used to master the 5 footer. Raise the ramp in two- to three-inch increments and begin with a single cut. Once you get the feel of the extra incline, move to a three-quarter cut and so on. The process remains the same until you are jumping on the Pro Tour with the 6-foot wall.

A drill that is sometimes helpful in learning the timing of the kick at higher speed, without the effort and danger of a full cut, is the high-speed fly over. Have the driver drive 5 to 10 mph faster than your normal jumping speed. Take a single-wake cut at the ramp. This will help you do two things: adapt to setting an edge at higher speed and react to the ramp as you approach it at greater speed.

What advice can the pros offer as you enter the ranks of the jumping elite? Freddy Krueger, known as the Deuce for consistently jumping 200-plus, told me the other day that "70 percent of jumping is having the guts to wait later and cut harder. The other 30 percent is using your brains so you stay alive."

TROUBLESHOOTING ADVANCED JUMPS

One advantage jumpers have over those competing in other events is that they get three attempts to go as far as they can. This means they have the opportunity to diagnose problems on the water, make adjustments, and cut at the ramp again. To help you make the correct adjustment, here are a few common errors and the corrections you should make.

PROBLEM: Slipping out to the left.

Cause: This is a result of flattening your skis at the base of the ramp and letting the boat pull your shoulders toward the boat.

Solution: You should concentrate on edging through the ramp and resisting the boat's pull by keeping the handle down and the shoulders parallel with the skis.

PROBLEM: Skis splitting on the ramp.

Cause: If you have the skis too far apart as you approach the ramp, the legs are in a weak position. This prevents you from resisting the ramp. Instead, the impact force of the ramp causes the skis to split apart.

Solution: Keep the skis closer together during the cut to the ramp so the legs are in a strong position to push off the ramp.

PROBLEM: Losing control or jumping the wakes.

Cause: It is easy to lose angle through the wakes because that is where the strongest pull from the boat is. Often, a skier will shift his or her weight to the left ski for balance across the wakes, but that is the exact opposite of what you should do.

Solution: Push the skis, especially the right one, onto edge more by driving the right knee down and across course toward the ramp.

PROBLEM: Crushing (inadvertent).

Cause: The lower body crush is caused by the skier having the knees flexed too much at the base of the ramp. The force of impact is so great that the legs are not able to respond quickly enough and they buckle underneath the skier.

Solution: Get the knees in the proper 90-degree bend so they can resist the ramp with a quick extension of the legs. This will lead to a springing lift off the ramp's surface.

PROBLEM: Upper body crush.

Cause: Having the legs too straight at the base of the ramp with the shoulders down and the back hunched over causes the lifting forces to be absorbed by the upper body. This is a dangerous position because it can lead to the dreaded OTF, out the front, the most painful of all jump crashes.

Solution: To prevent this disaster, flex the knees more and keep the back straight by pulling the handle down lower and closer to the body. Keep your head up and focus your eyes on the left corner of the ramp or into the horizon as you approach the base of the ramp. The upper body must remain calm, still, and erect so that the explosive power of the legs can lift the entire body up and off into flight.

PROBLEM: Slipping backward.

Cause: The out the back is caused by having your weight on your heels or sitting back too far as you approach the base of the ramp. This often happens when you are too early and flatten your skis off into the ramp.

Solution: If you are early and are flattening out your skis, turn later and slower, and hold your edge through the ramp. Always shift your weight to your toes before you start your turn. Press your knees and ankles into the skis as you initiate the turn.

The top jumpers all stress the same things—stay aggressive, edge through the ramp, keep your weight on your right ski, and keep your eyes and head up. The result is a jump like you see in figure 7.21. When you develop a solid foundation and the skills needed to edge through the ramp, you'll perform jumps like this too.

Figure 7.21   Build a solid foundation, and you'll be on your way to big jumps.

CHAPTER 8

COMPETITION

So you're interested in competition? If you're about to get your feet wet in a local competition for the first time, this chapter will provide some helpful information. If you're already a seasoned tournament competitor, read on. We've compiled a few interesting tips for you, too.

USA WATER SKI, INC.

The national governing body of water skiing is USA Water Ski, Inc., located in Winter Haven, Florida. USAWS, a member of the United States Olympic Committee, promotes the sport of water skiing and develops the rules of competition. The American Water Ski Association (AWSA) was recognized as a sport division under the reorganization of USAWS in early 1997. USAWS has divided water skiing into several sport divisions: water skiing (which includes slalom, tricks, and jump), kneeboarding, speed skiing, barefooting, collegiate, show skiing, disabled skiing, and soon, wakeboarding. Each division has its own set of rules and divisions of competition. Because this book has focused primarily on water skiing, we'll cover those rules in greater depth than those of the other divisions. If you would like to know more about the rules of competition for any division or event, you can buy an official rule book from USAWS by calling 941-324-4341. USAWS is a great resource to use if you are trying to install a course, develop a ski site, or learn more about the world of skiing.

AWSA COMPETITIVE AGE DIVISIONS

Water skiing competition breaks down into 11 divisions for both men and women. The age cutoffs are determined by your age on January 1 of the year that begins the day after the National Championships (held in mid-August each year). The divisions are given in table 8.1.

SLALOM

The object in slalom is to round as many buoys as possible without falling or missing a buoy or gate. The boat travels in a straight path down the center of the course, and the skier makes a serpentine path through the entrance gates, around each of the six skier buoys, and out through the exit gates. A minimum starting speed and a maximum speed is set for each division, as shown in table 8.2.

The skier selects the speed at which he or she wishes to start (only even speeds are allowed) and runs the course, with the speed being increased by 2 mph after each successful pass. When the skier reaches the maximum speed the rope is shortened from the standard 75-foot length to a 60-foot length (15 off). This shortening continues until the skier misses a buoy or falls. The cutoffs are preset loops in the rope that are the same for all divisions and tournaments. The shortening loops are located in the increments shown in figure 8.1.

Table 8.1   AWSA Age Divisions

Division	Ages
Boys/Girls I	9 years and under
Boys/Girls II	12 years and under
Boys/Girls III	13–16 years inclusive
Men/Women I	17–24 years inclusive
Men/Women II	25–34 years inclusive
Men/Women III	35–44 years inclusive
Men/Women IV	45–54 years inclusive
Men/Women V	55–64 years inclusive
Men/Women VI	65–74 years inclusive
Men/Women VII	75 years and over
Open Men/Women	Any age

Note: Rules are updated each year. Check the AWSA rule book for the latest information.

Table 8.2   Slalom Speeds

Division	Minimum	Maximum	Division	Minimum	Maximum
Boys I	16	30	Girls I	16	30
Boys II	26	34	Girls II	24	34
Boys III	30	36	Girls III	26	34
Men I	30	36	Women I	26	34
Men II	30	36	Women II	26	34
Men III	28	34	Women III	26	34
Men IV	28	34	Women IV	26	34
Men V	28	34	Women V	24	32
Men VI	26	32	Women VI	22	30
Men VII	24	30	Women VII	22	30
Open Men	30	36	Open Women	26	34

Note: Rules are updated each year. Check the AWSA rule book for the latest information.

Figure 8.2 gives the dimensions of a slalom course. Call USAWS for information on how to install a course.

TRICKS

In a tournament each skier has two 20-second passes to perform as many tricks as possible. Each trick is assigned a point value determined by its difficulty, and the skier who scores the most points is the winner. Table 8.3 gives the trick point values. The 20-second pass begins when the skier starts the first trick, at a point anywhere between the two course buoys. The skier may start at the yellow first buoy, and must start before reaching the orange second buoy because the clock will begin even if the skier has not started the first trick. Figure 8.3 gives the dimensions of an official trick course. The skier selects the boat speed, and the driver must maintain that speed for the entire course.

JUMP

The mission of every jumper is the same—to jump the farthest. The one who flies the farthest and skis away is the winner. You get three tries to push your distance out where no one can reach it. The maximum boat

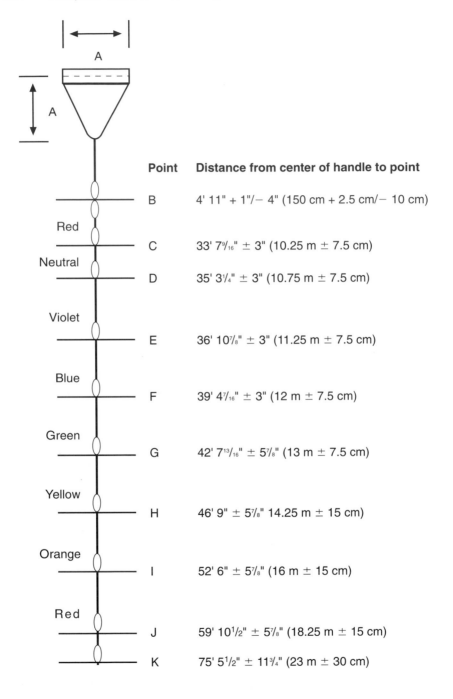

Point	Distance from center of handle to point
B	4' 11" + 1"/− 4" (150 cm + 2.5 cm/− 10 cm)
C	33' 7$^9/_{16}$" ± 3" (10.25 m ± 7.5 cm)
D	35' 3$^1/_4$" ± 3" (10.75 m ± 7.5 cm)
E	36' 10$^7/_8$" ± 3" (11.25 m ± 7.5 cm)
F	39' 4$^7/_{16}$" ± 3" (12 m ± 7.5 cm)
G	42' 7$^{13}/_{16}$" ± 5$^7/_8$" (13 m ± 7.5 cm)
H	46' 9" ± 5$^7/_8$" 14.25 m ± 15 cm)
I	52' 6" ± 5$^7/_8$" (16 m ± 15 cm)
J	59' 10$^1/_2$" ± 5$^7/_8$" (18.25 m ± 15 cm)
K	75' 5$^1/_2$" ± 11$^3/_4$" (23 m ± 30 cm)

Note: Handle assembly dimension A shall be 11" ± 1" (28 cm ± 4 cm) for tournament supplied handles only.

Figure 8.1   Slalom towline dimensions.   Courtesy of the American Water Ski Association.

Dimensions

Overall
length   259 m (849' 8⅞")
A   27 m (88' 7")
B   41 m (134' 6⅛")
C   29.347 m (96' 3⅜")
D   47.011 (154' 2¾")
E   1.25 m (4' 1¼")
F   11.5 m (37' 8¾")
G   1.15 m (3' 9¼")

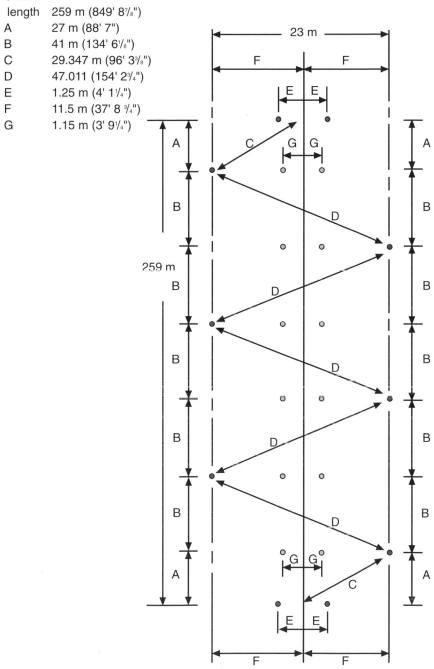

Figure 8.2   Official slalom course.   Courtesy of the American Water Ski Association.

Table 8.3   Trick Point Values

| | Water turns | | | | Wake turns | | | |
Description	No.	Code	2	1	No.	Code	2	1
Side slide	1	S	20*	40*				
Toehold side slide	2	TS		130*				
180° FB	3	B	30*	60*	14	WB	50*	80*
180° BF	4	F	30*	60*	15	WF	50*	80*
360° FF	5	O	40*	90*	16	WO	110*	150*
360° BB		BB	40*	90*	17	WBB	110*	150*
540° FB		5B	50	110	18	W5B	310*	310*
540° BF		5F	50	110	19	W5F	310*	310*
720° FF		7F	60	130	20	W7F	800*	800*
720° BB		7B	60	130	21	W7B	480*	480*
900° FB					22	W9B	850*	850*
900° BF						W9F	850*	850*
Stepover 180° FB	6	LB	70*	110	23	WLB	110*	160
Stepover 180° BF	7	LF	70*	110	24	WLF	110*	160
Stepover 360° FF					25	WLO	200*	260*
Stepover 360° BB					26	WLBB	200*	260*
Stepover 540° FB					27	WL5B	300*	420*
Double stepover 540° FB				500*		WL5LB		
Stepover 720° FF					27A	WL7F	700*	700*
Stepover 900° FB					27B	WL9B	800*	800*
Stepover 540° BF					28	WL5F	300*	420*
Double stepover 540° BF				500*		WL5LF		
Stepover 720° BB						WL7B	550*	550*
Stepover 900° BF					28A	WL9F	800*	800*
Toehold 180° FB	8	TB		100*	29	TWB		150*
Toehold 180° BF	9	TF		100*	30	TWF		150*
Toehold 360° FF	10	TO		200*	31	TWO		300*
Toehold 360° BB	11	TBB		200*	32	TWBB		330*
Toehold 540° FB	12	T5B		350*	33	TW5B		500*
Toehold 720° FF		T7F		450	35	TW7F		650*
Toehold 540° BF	13	T5F		350	34	TW5F		500
Toehold 720° BB					36	TW7B		650
Toehold stepover 180° FB					37	TWLB		320
Toehold stepover 180° BF					38	TWLF		380
Toehold stepover 360° FF					39	TWLO		480*

	Water turns				Wake turns			
	Trick		blue		Trick		skis	
Description	No.	Code	2	1	No.	Code	2	1
Toehold stepover 360° BB					40	TWLBB		480*
Toehold stepover 540° FB					41	TWL5B		600*
Toehold stepover 540° BF					42	TWL5F		700
Somersault forward					43	WflipF	800	800
Somersault backward					44	WflipB	500*	500*
Wake double flip					45	WDflip	1000	1000
Wake flip back full twist FF					46	WflipBFl	800	800
Wake flip back full twist BB						WflipBBBT	800	800
Wake flip back half twist FB					47	WflipBFB	750*	750*
Wake flip back line back						WflipBLB	800	800
Ski line 180° FB					48	SLB		350*
Ski line 180° BF					49	SLF		400*
Ski line 360° FF					50	SLO		400*
Ski line 360° BB					51	SLBB		450*
Ski line 540° FB					52	SL5B		550*
Ski line 540° BF					53	SL5F		550*
Ski line 720° BB					54	SL7B		750*
Ski line 720° FF					55	SL7F		800*

*Denotes tricks with allowable reverses. Reverses are the same value as basic trick.

Note: Trick point values are updated each year. Contact the AWSA for the current list.

Courtesy of the American Water Ski Association

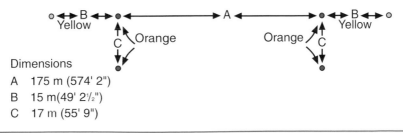

Dimensions
A   175 m (574' 2")
B   15 m(49' 2½")
C   17 m (55' 9")

Figure 8.3   Official trick course.   Courtesy of the American Water Ski Association

speed and ramp height are determined by the division in which you compete; however, the skier can elect to jump on a lower ramp, 5-foot minimum, or go a slower speed. Boys III, Men I, Men II, and Open Women have the option to jump on a 5+ foot ramp if they feel they can safely handle the taller ramp. Open Men jump on a 6-foot ramp. Men I, Men II, and Open Men jump at the maximum speed of 35 mph. Open Women, Women I and II, Boys III, and Girls III jump at 32 mph. Men III, IV, V, VI, and VII, and Women III, IV, and V jump at 30 mph. Women VI and VII, Boys II, and Girls II jump at 28 mph. Check the current AWSA rule book for the latest information because rules are updated each year.

Figure 8.4 gives the dimensions of an official jump course. You must ride the jump out past the ride-out buoys to get credit for the jump distance. If you're interested in purchasing or building a jump, give USAWS a call. They can set you up with plans on how to build a ramp or provide information about buying one.

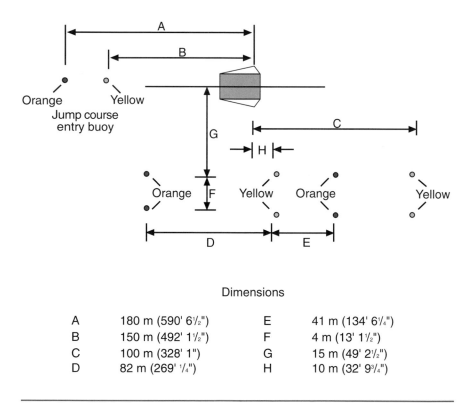

Dimensions

A	180 m (590' 6½")	E	41 m (134' 6¼")
B	150 m (492' 1½")	F	4 m (13' 1½")
C	100 m (328' 1")	G	15 m (49' 2½")
D	82 m (269' ¼")	H	10 m (32' 9¾")

Figure 8.4   Official jump course.   Courtesy of the American Water Ski Association

TIMING

In competition all events are timed to make sure the boat is going the same speed or the speed requested by the skier. If you're serious about training or really want to get into competition skiing, learning how to time the boat and drive at correct speeds is essential. USAWS is a great resource for information about proper times and speeds for all events and divisions. Most tournaments and many competition skiers use automatic electronic timers to ensure accuracy. This device is a great convenience for both the skier and the driver. It is amazing how far off you can be with hand timing. Several manufacturers make timing devices. The Pro Tour and many pro skiers currently use the Accu Ski model, but other manufacturers also build excellent timing systems. Call Accu Ski at 407-363-0354 for more information on automatic timers and new speed control devices to ensure consistency.

KNEEBOARDING

Kneeboarders also compete in three events: slalom, tricks, and flip offs. The kneeboard slalom course is a narrower version of a regulation course, and the minimum and maximum speeds are lower. The idea is the same—run as many buoys as possible. Kneeboarders do tricks in nearly the same fashion, from a conceptual standpoint, as traditional trickers do. Some tricks are different, however, and the point values are different. A sampling of kneeboard point values is given in table 8.4. The flip off is simply seeing who can do the most flips in a given amount of time, usually 20 seconds.

WAKEBOARDING

To win in wakeboarding you must not only do the high-point tricks but do them with style and intensity. As in tricking, point values are assigned to tricks based on difficulty, but you are also scored on how well you do them. You get two 25-second passes to perform five tricks per pass plus a wild-card trick at the end of the second pass to boost your style points or invent new tricks. With wakeboarding, riders focus on getting big air on each of the 10 highest point tricks they can do, whereas tricking skiers move quickly from trick to trick to get more points. Table 8.5 gives the point values and descriptions of surface wakeboard tricks. Some of the names sound a bit funky, but if you know anything about snowboarding or skateboarding they'll make more sense. The tricks

Table 8.4   Kneeboard Point Values

Description	Code	Value
Side slide*	S	20
Front to back*	B	30
Back to front*	F	30
360 Front to front*	O	40
360 Back to back*	OB	40
540 Front to back	5B	50
540 Back to front	5F	50
720 Front to front	7F	60
720 Back to back	7B	60
Air back*	AB	50
Air front*	AF	50
Wake back*	WB	100
Wake front*	WF	100
Air 360 back*	AOB	200
Wake 360*	WO	220
Wake 360 back*	WOB	320
Surface roll right	SRR	400
Surface roll left	SRL	400
Back roll right	BRR	400
Back roll left	BRL	400
Front roll right	FRR	450
Front roll left	FRL	450
Front somersault	FS	450
Wake 540 back*	W5B	500
Wake 540 front*	W5F	500
Back somersault	BS	500

*Denotes tricks with allowable reverses.

Note: Kneeboard point values are updated each year. Contact the American Kneeboard Association (AKA) for a complete list of current point values.

Courtesy of the American Water Ski Association

listed are intended only to whet your appetite; many more wakeboard tricks are currently being done in competition and by recreational wakeboarders.

AWSA RATING SYSTEM

The AWSA has developed two rating systems—one for those just learning to ski and a separate system for competitive skiers. Both systems are based on performance standards that correspond to a rating level. The AWSA is now developing a third rating system for intermediate skiers who aren't yet at the competitive level. The system should be completed soon.

Table 8.5   Wakeboard Point Values for Basic/Surface Tricks

FS/BS slalom turn (outside the wake)	50
FS/BS off the wake	50
Lipslide (boardslide on the lip of the wake)	100
FS/BS air (1 wake)	100
FS/BS surface 180	125
FS/BS off the wake 180	150
FS/BS olé 180 (rope goes over head)	150
Layback (rider lies back into the water)	200
Hang five (five toes over nose of board)	200
FS/BS surface 360	200
FS/BS off the wake 360	250
FS/BS olé 360	275
FS/BS air (2 wake)	250
Butt slide (hold for 1 sec minimum)	250
Butt slide with rail grab	300
Fin release (slalom turn with fin out)	300
FS/BS line cutter 360 (board goes over rope)	350
Body slide (hold for 1 sec minimum)	350
Body slide with fin release	400
High speed butt slide (board out of water, 1 sec minimum, 28 mph)	400
Backscratcher (board raised at least 90° angle to water, no grab)	400
The Bain (combo bunny hop 180° with olé 180—continuous move)	400
Perez (slalom turn into surface 360)	450
Troy tumble (high speed butt slide with tumble turn)	550
Tumple turn (at normal boat speed)	700

Notes: FS = frontside, BS = backside
Wakeboard point values are updated each year. Contact USAWS for a complete list of current point values.

Courtesy of the American Water Ski Association

The Learn to Ski Challenge is for the first-time through intermediate skier. It breaks the process of learning to ski into small, achievable goals, and the skier receives an achievement sticker upon achieving the skill. It's a great way to track improvement and establish goals for skiing. For more information and the required forms for the Learn to Ski Challenge, call or write USAWS.

The competition system establishes performance standards for each event. The 2nd Class, 1st Class, and Expert ratings can be earned in practice, but an AWSA-certified judge must witness the performance. Skiers must earn Masters, EP (exceptional performance), and Open ratings in a USAWS-sanctioned tournament. The performance standards for the competitive rating system are given in tables 8.6 for females and 8.7 for males.

Table 8.6   AWSA Performance Ratings—Females[1]

Division	Event	EP	Master	Expert	1st Class	2nd Class	NOPS[2] EP
Girls I	Slalom	34 buoys 4@26 mph	23 buoys 1@26 mph	12 buoys 18 mph	4 buoys 4@16 mph	2 buoys 2@16 mph	945
	Tricks	560	320	240	160	40	
Girls II	Slalom	35 buoys 5@34 mph	25 buoys 1@32 mph	14 buoys 2@28 mph	4 buoys 4@24 mph	2 buoys 2@24 mph	995
	Tricks	1,400	740	320	240	160	
	Jump	42-28-5	37-28-5	30-28-5	25-28-5	20-28-5	
Girls III	Slalom	44 buoys 2@14.25 m	39 buoys 3@16 m	25 buoys 1@34 mph	20 buoys 2@32 mph	6 buoys 6@26 mph	1,674
	Tricks	2,000	1,600	850	450	320	
	Jump	92-32-5	79-32-5	53-32-5	41-32-5	35-32-5	
Women I	Slalom	46 buoys 4@14.25 m	42 buoys 6@16 m	23 buoys 5@32 mph	14 buoys 2@30 mph	3 buoys 3@26 mph	1,982
	Tricks	2,200	1,900	1,000	650	320	
	Jump	98-32-5	80-32-5	50-32-5	40-32-5	37-32-5	
Women II	Slalom	43 buoys 1@14.25 m	35 buoys 5@18.25 m	23 buoys 5@32 mph	15 buoys 3@30 mph	8 buoys 2@28 mph	1,985
	Tricks	2,000	1,500	940	650	320	
	Jump	89-32-5	77-32-5	45-32-5	39-32-5	35-32-5	
Women III	Slalom	40 buoys 4@16 m	38 buoys 2@16 m	22 buoys 4@32 mph	15 buoys 3@30 mph	4 buoys 4@26 mph	1,586
	Tricks	2,300	1,500	940	650	320	
	Jump	76-30-5	70-30-5	45-30-5	34-30-5	21-30-5	
Women IV	Slalom	30 buoys 6@34 mph	27 buoys 3@34 mph	18 buoys 6@30 mph	14 buoys 2@30 mph	3 buoys 3@26 mph	1,297
	Tricks	1,400	1,000	850	650	320	
	Jump	55-30-5	50-30-5	45-30-5	34-30-5	30-30-5	
Women V	Slalom	29 buoys 5@32 mph	22 buoys 4@30 mph	12 buoys 6@26 mph	6 buoys 6@24 mph	2 buoys 2@24 mph	1,569
	Tricks	1,100	740	560	450	320	
	Jump	50-30-5	46-30-5	40-30-5	32-30-5	25-30-5	
Women VI	Slalom	25 buoys 1@30 mph	16 buoys 4@26 mph	12 buoys 6@24 mph	6 buoys 6@22 mph	2 buoys 2@22 mph	1,595
	Tricks	650	540	450	320	160	
	Jump	40-28-5	35-28-5	30-28-5	25-28-5	20-28-5	
Women VII	Slalom	14 buoys 2@26 mph	10 buoys 4@24 mph	8 buoys 2@24 mph	4 buoys 4@22 mph	2 buoys 2@22 mph	1,557
	Tricks	540	320	240	160	40	
	Jump	30-28-5	25-28-5	23-28-5	20-28-5	15-28-5	
Women Open Ratings	Slalom	57 buoys (3@12 m)					
	Tricks	5,500					
	Jump	122-32-5 117-30-5					

Notes: [1]Ratings for 1996-97
[2]National Overall Performance Standards
Courtesy of the American Water Ski Association

Table 8.7   AWSA Performance Ratings—Males[1]

Division	Event	EP	Master	Expert	1st Class	2nd Class	NOPS[2] EP
Boys I	Slalom	47 buoys 5@30 mph	30 buoys 6@24 mph	18 buoys 6@20 mph	4 buoys 4@18 mph	2 buoys 2@18 mph	1,264
	Tricks	740	560	320	240	120	
Boys II	Slalom	41 buoys 5@16 m	26 buoys 2@34 mph	17 buoys 5@30 mph	4 buoys 4@26 mph	2 buoys 2@26 mph	1,343
	Tricks	1,500	940	560	320	240	
	Jump	79-28-5	55-28-5	45-28-5	35-28-5	31-28-5	
Boys III	Slalom	46 buoys 4@13 m	35 buoys 5@16 m	18 buoys 6@34 mph	9 buoys 3@32 mph	2 buoys 2@30 mph	1,897
	Tricks	3,000	1,600	850	560	320	
	Jump	121-32-5	108-32-5	76-32-5	57-32-5	45-32-5	
Men I	Slalom	51 buoys 3@12 m	44 buoys 2@13 m	32 buoys 2@16 m	17 buoys 5@34 mph	5 buoys 5@30 mph	1,884
	Tricks	3,800	1,900	940	740	560	
	Jump	145-35-5½	121-35-5½	96-35-5½	75-35-5½	54-35-5½	
Men II	Slalom	50 buoys 2@12 m	41 buoys 5@14.25 m	23 buoys 5@36 mph	17 buoys 5@34 mph	7 buoys 1@32 mph	1,903
	Tricks	3,100	1,400	940	560	320	
	Jump	135-35-5½	114-35-5½	89-35-5½	67-35-5½	54-35-5½	
Men III	Slalom	54 buoys 6@12 m	46 buoys 4@13 m	40 buoys 4@14.25 m	33 buoys 3@16 m	17 buoys 5@32 mph	2,088
	Tricks	3,000	1,900	940	740	320	
	Jump	118-32-5	102-32-5	84-32-5	62-32-5	50-32-5	
Men IV	Slalom	50 buoys 2@12 m	44 buoys 2@13 m	35 buoys 5@16 m	21 buoys 3@34 mph	6 buoys 6@28 mph	2,243
	Tricks	2,600	1,600	940	650	320	
	Jump	100-30-5	89-30-5	67-30-5	48-30-5	38-30-5	
Men V	Slalom	40 buoys 4@14.25 m	35 buoys 5@16 m	12 buoys 6@30 mph	8 buoys 2@30 mph	4 buoys 4@28 mph	1,877
	Tricks	1,700	1,400	940	650	320	
	Jump	78-30-5	70-30-5	56-30-5	51-30-5	38-30-5	
Men VI	Slalom	34 buoys 4@16 m	26 buoys 2@18.25 m	16 buoys 4@30 mph	8 buoys 2@28 mph	4 buoys 4@26 mph	1,682
	Tricks	940	650	320	240	160	
	Jump	51-30-5	46-30-5	40-30-5	35-30-5	30-30-5	
Men VII	Slalom	20 buoys 2@30 mph	12 buoys 6@26 mph	8 buoys 2@26 mph	4 buoys 4@24 mph	2 buoys 2@24 mph	1,650
	Tricks	540	320	240	160	40	
	Jump	30-30-5	25-30-5	23-30-5	20-30-5	15-30-5	
Men Open Ratings	Slalom	57 buoys (3@11.25 m @ 36 mph) 59 buoys (5@11.25 m @ 34 mph)					
	Tricks	7,000					
	Jump	176-35-6/168-35-5½/141-32-5/132-30-5					

Notes: [1]Ratings for 1996-97
[2]National Overall Performance Standards
Courtesy of the American Water Ski Association

ENTERING A TOURNAMENT

How do you find out when and where tournaments are being held? USAWS publishes a regional directory of all the tournaments held in each of five regions in the United States. Call USAWS, join up, and ask them for a copy of the guide for your region. When you get the guide, look through it to find the date, time, entry fee, and deadline, and mail in your entry.

I suggest skiing in an F (for fun-sanctioned) tournament or a novice tournament your first time out. Many ski clubs host these types of tournaments, and water skiing leagues and novice tours are sweeping the country. These tournaments are great for weekend skiers who want to see how they measure up against the local competition.

To make sure your first experience is enjoyable, find out when your event is being held and get there at least two hours before it starts. Take the time to introduce yourself to the judges and skiers. You'll find that they are a friendly bunch. They are excited by new skiers and will help you learn the ropes and make your first tournament a success, no matter how you ski. Don't be intimidated! Everyone has a first tournament, and most of us will try to help the new kid whenever we can.

I remember my first tournament quite well. I crashed in jump, missed my first trick, and didn't get to the #2 ball in slalom. Few, if any, have had a worse tournament. I think I set a new record low overall score. I was nervous, I didn't know a soul there, and I was embarrassed to near death. Your first tournament can be a nightmare like mine, or it can be a great time no matter how you ski. It all depends on your attitude and your goals. A great goal for a first tournament is to have fun, meet new people, and learn from the experience. If you ski well—great, that's a bonus. If you don't, no need to feel discouraged. It happens to us all.

TOURNAMENT TIPS

The lakes are full of skiers who can tear it up on their home site or in good conditions, but who, for some reason or another, fall apart when the pressure of a tournament hits them. Part of learning how to become a tournament skier is developing mental toughness to deal with adverse conditions and mental obstacles that block peak performances. We'll discuss the secrets of mental toughness in the next two chapters. The other part of becoming a tough tournament competitor is learning the strategies of how to ski in less-than-ideal conditions. We'll give you those insights now.

Wind

Light winds are a skier's friend. In slalom a light headwind gives the water texture, helps slow you down before the turn, and keeps the water flat. A light headwind in jump helps create lift. The trouble comes when the wind is too strong, or is blowing from behind you or across the course. The following sections provide tips about how to handle different types of wind in each event.

Slalom

- In a headwind, pull out later for the gates. Pull longer and stronger across the course. Try to set up to run your most difficult pass into the wind.
- In a tailwind, pull out earlier for the gates. Make your pull strong, but start your edge change sooner. Stay patient in the turn. Do the work behind the boat rather than during the turn.
- If a crosswind is blowing you away from the boat on the pullout, pull out earlier. If a crosswind is blowing you into the boat, pull out later. The secret is to pull long and strong into the headwind side of a crosswind and strong, but with a quick edge change, into the tailwind side.

Tricks

- In a headwind, the line will become tight sooner. Most top skiers prefer to do handle tricks into the wind.
- A tailwind will create a delay before the rope tightens after a trick. You have less pull from the boat; thus you need to wait longer for the rope before your next trick.
- Tricking in a crosswind is determined by which foot forward you are and which wake you like to use for your tricks. Use whatever feels best to you in this situation.

Jump

- The key to jumping in a headwind is to be comfortable coming down into the course farther before turning for the jump. You must pull stronger across the course and wait longer than usual.
- Tailwinds allow the jumper to get wider on the boat; thus you must turn sooner for the ramp and maintain a strong edge through the ramp. If you don't get wider, you must wait longer because the wind will give you increased acceleration across the course.
- If a crosswind is blowing you away from the jump, you must turn earlier for the ramp and focus on skiing across course. This wind

blows you into the ramp on landings, so getting back into a skiing position quickly is essential. If a crosswind is blowing you into the ramp, you must make a later cut to the ramp.

Rollers

Rough or rolling water poses another problem for skiers. Two things to focus on when skiing in these conditions are knee bend and eye focus. In rough water it's essential to lower your center of gravity and stay in a low position by flexing your knees in the turns. Use your knees as shock absorbers to smooth out the rollers or rough water. To keep your balance in such conditions keep your head up and your eyes focused on the horizon. Another trick to skiing slalom in rough water is to ski as early and wide as possible so you can keep both hands on the handle longer in the turns. That way you have more time to make controlled, smooth turns rather than rushing things.

CHAPTER 9

MENTAL TOUGHNESS AND TRAINING STRATEGIES

You have heard it before. You have probably said it yourself: "It's all mental" or "Skiing is 90 percent mental." Most athletes will acknowledge that 60 to 90 percent of success in their sport is because of mental toughness. In spite of this, very few recreational or competitive athletes regularly practice mental skills or mental toughness. So what is mental training? Kay Porter, PhD and Judy Foster, in *Mental Training for Peak Athletic Performance,* define mental training as learning and practicing psychological skills to enhance athletic performance. Mental training is not a "silver bullet" that will solve all your problems; it is part of your talent foundation that works with your fitness training, skiing training, and proper dietary habits to make you the best you can be. But how important is mental toughness? Olympic gold medalist Bruce Jenner said this, "I always felt that my greatest asset was not my physical ability—it was my mental ability." The same sentiment has been expressed by other superathletes such as Jack Nicklaus, Pele, Bruce Lee, and Billie Jean King. Given their record of achievement, read on and learn the secrets to mental toughness.

Every skier accumulates a wealth of knowledge from individual experience. Most performances, especially from younger athletes, tend to resemble a roller coaster, with highs and lows. How do athletes eliminate the bad performances so that they can perform well all the time? Athletes must reflect and learn from their mistakes, take control of the outcomes, and prepare for positive results. If you can learn what makes you tick, you can let people around you know what you need (for example, support or advice) to help you perform to your full potential. You can accomplish this by getting to know what factors contribute to poor performances and what factors contribute to good performances.

PEAK-PERFORMANCE FACTORS

Researchers have identified a number of factors that significantly influence athletic performance. We can classify these into seven critical areas: goal setting, practice habits, mental rehearsal, focus of energy, intensity management, attention control, and thought control. For your convenience, we have filtered through the mass of sport psychology research and pulled together the information that will be most helpful to you in developing an effective mental toughness training program. Following is a brief description of each of the performance factors. Read through each factor and consider how it may be affecting you and your progress in skiing.

1. Goal Setting

When eastern European sport psychology researchers studied the difference between athletic champions and average athletes, they discovered two important and significant differences. The first is that the champions do not just set goals, they write them down. The second is that they visualize themselves accomplishing their goals. In this section we will discuss the power of setting goals. Visualizing the attainment of the goal will come later. Motivational speaker Don Hutson discusses data showing that less than one half of one percent of the population have written goals. Furthermore, Hutson reveals that when you write down your goal, you have a 300 percent greater probability of attaining it. So let's take some time to learn how to set and write down your goals.

Goal setting is establishing specific short- and long-range goals for your skiing that are realistic, challenging, and measurable. Top skiers establish effective goals and objectives that guide their training programs day to day, week to week, and month to month. By establishing goals and objectives, these skiers prevent slumps and performance plateaus and remain on a steady course of improvement.

Types of Goals.   In athletic training a goal is much more than just winning. It is any future objective that you wish for. Goals are a very powerful way to focus your mind and motivate you for the things you want from your athletic and personal life. Goals help you establish a consistent program for training and competition that will aid in preparing you for competition and prevent overtraining. There are five types of goals that you should set:

- Long-term goals: what you ultimately want to achieve in skiing and in your personal life (for example, become a world champion).
- Seasonal goals: what you want to achieve this season (for example, place in the top five at nationals).
- Competitive goals: how you want to perform in specific tournaments during the season (for example, run 3 at 35 in regionals).
- Training goals: what you need to do in your fitness, skiing, mental training, and diet that will enable you to reach your competitive goals (for example, work out twice per week).
- Lifestyle goals: what you need to alter in your lifestyle to reach the stated goals (for example, stop drinking alcohol).

Many skiers mistakenly believe they are setting a goal when they exclaim, "My goal is to finish in the top three at regionals" or, "I'd like to win at least two tournaments this year." Although such wishes or desires are important milestones by which to judge progress, these long-term desires serve as motivation to train hard rather than specific goals to guide daily training. Goal setting refers to measurable improvements—for example, the number of buoys you improve in a year, the number of new tricks you learn, and even more important, what you intend to do each week to achieve these goals. This is the essence of goal setting. Identifying ahead of time the actual steps that you will take to move toward your goal is what will allow you to accomplish your dreams.

SMART Guidelines.   Before we go any further, let's learn to use the **SMART** guidelines and get your goals on paper.

Specific—Set goals that are specific, not general. Rather than starting with "I want to improve my trick run," you should set a goal of improving your trick run by, for example, learning two new tricks and eliminating a specific error, perhaps straight knees, that exists in your present run.

Measurable—Establish goals that are quantifiable and measurable. Determine by how much you would like to improve. For example, a jumper's goal may be to increase his or her distance by an average of 15 feet with no more than 10 percent of jumps shorter than 120 feet.

Attainable—Design goals that are challenging, yet attainable. Your goals should be realistic given your time frame and physical ability.

Recorded—Record all your goals in your training log. Track your progress toward your goals and monitor whether you need to revise your goals during the season based on your rate of progress.

Timelined—You should project the achievement of all goals within a predetermined period. Preferably, you should divide your goals into minigoals that guide your progress throughout the year. The idea is to have constant, small successes that keep you motivated to work toward your long-term goals. Suppose you are presently a mid-28-off skier and your long-term performance goal is to run 32 off. You set a minigoal of running 28 off by the end of next month. Don Hutson tells us that "there are no impossible goals, only impossible time frames."

Figure 9.1   Set specific goals, such as learning a new trick, not general ones.

Performance, Process, and Practice Goals. Top skiers establish three types of goals for both the long term and the current season: performance goals, process goals, and practice goals.

> **Performance goals**—A desired result, such as top three at the club championships or 4 at 22 off.
>
> **Process goals**—The aspects of your training (for example, increasing leg strength by 10 percent, reducing your body fat percentage by 8 percent, or edging through the wakes) that you will improve to enhance your performance goals. These types of goals are sometimes referred to as lifestyle goals because they indicate what physical, technical, mental, and nutritional changes you need to make in your general lifestyle to reach your performance goals.
>
> **Practice goals**—Day-to-day activities (for example, weight training, supervised drills, coached lessons) that you will conduct to achieve your process goals. These goals specify which strategies you will use in your physical, technical, mental, and nutritional training to accomplish your process goals.

Take the time right now to fill out the worksheet on page 200. This is the first step toward achieving your goals in a manner that will provide you with a day-to-day, month-to-month plan. This approach will prevent slumps and performance plateaus and keep you on a steady course to the next level in your skiing ability.

If you are having difficulty with this exercise, it may be helpful to sit down with your coach or ski partner to assess which specific areas of your technical, mental, and physical skills directly affect your skiing performance. Fill out the performance evaluation on page 202 to help you focus on areas of weakness.

2. Practice Habits

Practice habits refer to the factors that contribute to successful training on and off the water. Top skiers have the self-discipline to get the most out of their practice time by practicing with a purpose, obtaining coaching, and constantly working on all the technical, mental, and fitness aspects of their skiing. Jack Nicklaus said it best, "Practice doesn't make perfect, perfect practice makes perfect." What is perfect practice? You can accomplish perfect practice only when you know exactly what it is that you are trying to achieve. It means you have a plan and specific skills you are trying to improve. When you get on the water or to the gym, you must already know the drills, exercises, or practice strategies you will execute during that training period. Many skiers use the ad

PERSONALIZED SUCCESS TRAINING PLAN

I. Performance goals: Desired scores, placements, skills

	Present level	Desired improvement	Completion date
Slalom	_____	_____	_____
Trick	_____	_____	_____
Jump	_____	_____	_____
Overall	_____	_____	_____
Wakeboard	_____	_____	_____

II. Process goals: To improve my skiing, I will improve my skills in these areas.

Technical skills

1. _____
2. _____
3. _____

Physical skills

1. _____
2. _____
3. _____

Mental toughness

1. _____
2. _____
3. _____

Nutrition

1. _____
2. _____
3. _____

III. Practice goals: To improve the above skills, I will implement the following strategies into my training.

Technical drills

1. _____
2. _____

3. _____

Physical workouts

1. _____

2. _____

3. _____

Mental toughness drills

1. _____

2. _____

3. _____

---

hoc training plan we discussed earlier. They begin skiing or working out and only then do they assess what they may need to work on. Rather than attempting to identify problems each time you practice, you should have a preestablished plan that dictates what you will accomplish each day. Perfect practice is simply having the self-discipline to develop and implement a plan according to your goals. Use the goal-setting exercise you completed and fill out a practice schedule like the one shown on page 204. This will become your map to success.

Ideally, you should schedule your training one month in advance so that you don't make daily changes without substantial data to guide you. By beginning now and committing to a specific training plan, you will increase your chances of making long-lasting, positive improvements in your skiing ability and skills.

Skiers will often spend valuable practice time socializing with friends or playing around. Although these activities may be enjoyable, challenging, and inviting, you must have the discipline to make practice your priority. Activities that are not part of your plan distract you from your course of progress. Do you socialize during practice? Do you spend time helping or coaching others when you should be training? How many minutes of quality time do you get on the water when you go out? Having fun and socializing with your friends is important, but if you are serious about achieving your goals, you must be serious about your practice. This disciplined approach to training allows you to achieve maximum skill development—your ultimate goal.

3. Mental Rehearsal

Mental rehearsal is your ability to practice, visualize, and feel your performance on the water before execution. As we noted in the

PERSONAL PERFORMANCE EVALUATION

Skier's name_____

Division _____ Age _____ Date _____

SLALOM SKILLS

Rate your performance (1-5) on each skill (5 = excellent).

BODY POSITION

Head and shoulders _____

Hips forward _____

Ankle and knees _____

ACCELERATION

Angle through wakes _____

Intensity of pull _____

Length of pull _____

DECELERATION

Edge change _____

Reach _____

Turn smoothness _____

TRICK SKILLS

Rate your performance (1-5) on each skill (5 = excellent).

TRICK: _____

Head position _____

Shoulder position _____

Knees (Flexibility) _____

Arm position _____

Handle control _____

Edge control _____

Timing on wake _____

Axis control _____

TRICK: _____

Head position _____

Shoulder position _____

Knees (Flexibility) _____

Arm position _____

Handle control _____

Edge control _____

Timing on wake _____

Axis control _____

TRICK: _____

Head position _____

Shoulder position _____

Knees (Flexibility) _____

Arm position _____

Handle control _____

Edge control _____

Timing on wake _____

Axis control _____

TRICK: _____

Head position _____

Shoulder position _____

Knees (Flexibility) _____

Arm position _____

Handle control _____

Edge control _____

Timing on wake _____

Axis control _____

JUMP SKILLS

Rate your performance (1-5) on each skill (5 = excellent).

COUNTER CUT
Head and eyes _____
Hips and shoulders _____
Arms and handle_____
Knees and ankles_____
Angle through wakes_____
Edge control_____

LIFT
Head and eyes _____
Hips and shoulders _____
Arms and handle_____
Knees and ankles_____
Angle through wakes_____
Edge control_____

TURN
Head and eyes _____
Hips and shoulders _____
Arms and handle _____
Knees and ankles _____
Angle through wakes _____
Edge control _____

LANDING
Head and eyes _____
Hips and shoulders _____
Arms and handle_____
Knees and ankles_____
Angle through wakes_____
Edge control_____

CUT TO RAMP
I lead and eyes _____
Hips and shoulders _____
Arms and handle_____

Knees and ankles_____
Angle through wakes_____
Edge control_____

MENTAL SKILLS

Rate your performance (1-5) on each skill (5 = excellent).

SLALOM
Emotional control _____
Attention control _____
Self confidence _____
Positive imagery _____
Motivation _____

JUMP
Emotional control _____
Attention control _____
Self confidence _____
Positive imagery _____
Motivation _____

TRICKS
Emotional control _____
Attention control _____
Self confidence _____
Positive imagery _____
Motivation _____

NOTES
_____
_____
_____
_____

PRACTICE SCHEDULE

My practice schedule for the above strategies will include

TECHNICAL SKILLS

Strategy 1_____ sessions/week for _____ minutes/session
Strategy 2_____ sessions/week for _____ minutes/session
Strategy 3_____ sessions/week for _____ minutes/session

PHYSICAL WORKOUT SKILLS

Strategy 1_____ sessions/week for _____ minutes/session
Strategy 2_____ sessions/week for _____ minutes/session
Strategy 3_____ sessions/week for _____ minutes/session

MENTAL TOUGHNESS SKILLS

Strategy 1_____ sessions/week for _____ minutes/session
Strategy 2_____ sessions/week for _____ minutes/session
Strategy 3_____ sessions/week for _____ minutes/session

---

goal-setting section, this is one of the two areas that separates the champions from the also-rans. Rehearsing an athletic activity in the mind's eye is a vital practice and competition strategy that has been scientifically proven to stimulate the muscles in proper sequence. Mental rehearsal acts as a warm-up for competition by alerting the muscles that will be used.

You will see additional benefits from mental rehearsal when learning a new motor skill. This supports the idea of skiers' rehearsing their performances away from the lake to improve consistency and learn new skills.

Visualization, watching a movie in your mind, is the most common form of mental rehearsal. Many skiers report that they engage in mental rehearsal even though they do not see pictures in their mind. These skiers rehearse the feelings they experience while skiing. Whether you see pictures or experience feelings is not important; what is significant is that you learn to rehearse in your mind before you compete and as you are learning new skills.

There are three views or angles from which to rehearse: (1) imagine you are on shore or in the boat watching an expert; (2) see yourself from the shore or the boat; and (3) see the view from your body as if you were actually on the water. Use whatever method works best for you. Begin by getting comfortable and in a relaxed, focused, day-dreaming mode. Lie down or sit somewhere where you won't be disturbed for 15 or 20 minutes. Take several deep breaths that fill your lungs with fresh air. Close your eyes and use the following imagery sequences for your particular event. Focus on these things as you go through each imagery sequence:

1. Get in tune with your senses. Feel the coolness of the water, smell the fresh air, see the colors of the trees, hear the rumble of the boat.
2. Trust your images and develop a feeling of confidence and control.
3. Use key anchor words to trigger positive feelings or images of success.
4. Make trouble spots easy by slowing down the images.

Slalom.   Start your set as you would in practice, from either the boat or the dock. Pull out for the gates and set up for the gate shot. Think of your turn and lean, the rope in relation to your body, the location of the boat, what your focus is. You are probably focusing on the #1 ball and the right-hand gate buoy. As you change edge into the first buoy, where are you looking? What is the position of your ski? See the water, the handle, the buoy. See yourself make a perfect turn around the #1 ball and cross the wakes with angle and perfect body position. Always be aware of your focus. See yourself make perfect turns and strong leans at every buoy. The time it takes is not important. For problem spots, or if your image is not perfect, slow it down to frame by frame and make any corrections necessary. The better you become, the more you will be able to speed up the image to real time. Finally, see yourself exit the gates and feel the exhilaration you feel in real life after every pass.

It is important to be accurate in what you see and to be aware of the feelings your body has with every movement. Be patient and consistent with developing these images. It takes practice. Concentrate on the quality of the imagery, not the quantity. You should practice this three or four times per week, running four or five passes. Begin with your starting speed or pass and then run through a pass at a personal-best performance. Never end your rehearsal in the middle of a pass.

Tricking and Boarding.   You are approaching the start of your first pass. See the boat in front of you, the wakes, your ski, the shore. Be aware of everything around you. As you start your tricks, be aware of your body position. See what you would see if you were really on the water. Make each trick smooth and perfect. Make your pass flow as it would if you were really doing it. Make sure there are no blank spots in your imagery. If there are, fill them in with what you should be seeing.

Stay focused on doing each trick flawlessly. Time is not a factor; keep it slow and perfect. As you begin to perfect each trick, you can time yourself to gauge if your imagery is realistic.

Perfection is the key. It takes time, but be patient. The work will pay off. Practice this three to four times per week, running each pass three times.

Jumping.   You are on the water, about to begin your first cut. From inside your body, see everything you see on the water—your skis, the boat, the ramp, your focus. Set your edge for your counter cut and see yourself power up to the side of the boat. See yourself make a perfect slow turn and drop your hip as you cut to the ramp. Notice your point of focus and see that your body position is perfect as you cross the wakes and generate controlled speed. See yourself get onto the ramp in perfect position. Feel the forces of the ramp and the power in your legs as you kick. Where is your point of focus? See yourself lift off the top of the ramp and elevate as you fly through the air. Feel your legs extend and feel the pull from the boat as it lifts you even higher. Notice your focus point. See the water and feel your body position as you prepare to land. Feel the impact of landing and see yourself absorb it. Stand up smoothly and under control, and ski out the jump.

If there is a certain spot where you don't feel confident or have some feelings of fear, don't worry. Simply slow everything down. Replay the area of concern until it is perfect and you are confident in your ability. As it becomes easier, speed it back up to real time. Do this exercise three or four times a week in sets of three to four jumps.

Difficult Areas, New Tricks, and Skills.   How do you learn a new skill, technique, or trick through imagery? How do you perfect skills or tricks, or eliminate the fear associated with a problem area?

Begin by watching a video of a top skier performing the skill perfectly. Now imagine watching the same skier from the shore. When you can see this, put yourself on the water and watch yourself from outside your body as you perform the skill perfectly. Once you perfect this, put yourself back inside your body and see what you would see when you perform the skill. Timing is very important. You must slow everything down to a frame-by-frame picture and be aware of everything you normally see—the boat, the shore, the rope. When you come to the difficult part or the area where you fall, go back to seeing yourself from outside your body and complete the skill. Force yourself to complete the skill perfectly, running it at slow motion. As you mentally perfect the skill, put it in with the flow of movements before and after the trouble area and begin to speed up to real time.

4. Focus of Energy

Focus of energy refers to the direction (positive or negative) in which you focus your mind while skiing. Skiers who concentrate on positive thoughts tend to stay optimistic regardless of poor performances, conditions, or uncontrollable events. Conversely, skiers with a negative focus of energy tend to be pessimistic while competing and are therefore aware of all the bad things that have happened to them or could happen to them.

Your focus of energy is a reflection of years of experience coping with successes and failures. Some skiers learn at a very early age that they need to stay positive regardless of the circumstances. These positive thinkers motivate themselves toward optimal performance by finding pleasure in reaching their short-term goals. Positive thinkers anticipate success and focus on their strength under pressure. They strive to be the best they can be every time they step on the water without regard for the possibility of failure. They view every situation as an opportunity to shine, not a threat of possible failure.

Research has conclusively shown that negative thinking can adversely affect performance. How does this happen? Any thoughts or feelings that disrupt the manner in which our bodies function can place undue stress on the nervous system. This will interfere directly with athletic performance. Do you have negative thoughts or reactions during competition or practice that result in your becoming angry, anxious, upset, or discouraged? These negative emotions may be the root of your inconsistent performance. Stabilizing your emotions can result in improved consistency and peak performance.

When their performance is less than stellar, skiers with a poor focus of energy often find themselves in a cycle of negative thinking. Coaches, parents, friends, and training partners often reinforce this downward spiral. Acting with good intentions, they encourage the skier to stay aware of mistakes so that he or she can attempt to keep them under control. The strategy of mistake management eventually catches up with the skier by undermining self-confidence and creating fear, concern, and tension during performances. To battle this, you must acknowledge that it is OK to expect great results and it is OK to applaud great efforts, even when the performance is less than your best. Such positive thinking does not lead to complacency, as many negative thinkers believe. Poor performances should simply lead to improved practice, not self-belittlement. Give yourself the best chance to succeed by always staying positive during competition and practice. This attitude is a prerequisite to becoming a champion.

If you have trouble with your focus of energy, use affirmations—positive self-statements about something that is true or has a realistic possibility of becoming true. Using affirmations can be a powerful strategy to shift to a more positive mindset and block out negative thoughts. With affirmations, you can change patterns of negative thought that, like tape recordings in your head, continue to play old, counterproductive tunes. Affirmations help you develop your full potential by replacing the old tape with a new, positive litany that can transform the quality of your life and improve your performances. Affirmations are always positive, they are personal to you, they are concisely stated in the present tense, and they begin with I. Some examples include the following:

"I am as good as any skier here today."
"I am confident and ready to win."
"I am the best. I will be the best."
"I have trained properly and am ready to win."

Some skiers like to make their affirmations rhyme so they remember them better.

"I'm in position to strike and get what I like."
"I ski to win when I ski within."

Some skiers have difficulty with affirmations. They feel they are deceiving themselves when they state something that may be true in the future but is not true now. A skier may have difficulty saying "I am a national champion" before he or she has actually won anything. What we all need to remember is that affirmations are not self-deception; they are self-direction. An affirmation is like a compass that puts you on the fastest path for your trip to success.

5. Thought Control

Thought control is closely related to focus of energy. It refers to your ability to minimize negative and unnecessary thoughts and to use positive thinking and intentions to your advantage. Signs of weak thought control include having an excessively active mind before competition or not being able to turn on your automatic pilot and trust your preparation. When asked what they were thinking during record-breaking performances, world-class skiers and other athletes often say, "I wasn't thinking anything. I just felt like I was in a zone and my body did whatever I wanted it to do." This feeling of performing without thoughts, trusting pretrained skills, and just letting it happen is common among elite athletes.

Less experienced skiers, on the other hand, often attempt to improve their performances with conscious control of their technical skills. Although these skiers may feel more in control mentally, they inadvertently create tension in their muscles that inhibits performance. Do you trust your skills enough to simply "do it your way," or do you feel a need to focus on your technique to ensure that nothing will break down? A strategy used by many skiers to learn to shift onto automatic pilot is progressive relaxation. This technique works very well with visualization and affirmation because it calms the mind and lets the thoughts and images sink into your subconscious. Premade tapes can help you learn this technique, also known as self-hypnosis. Here is a brief explanation of the process and an exercise to help you learn to calm your mind and get into the zone.

People learn progressive relaxation in three phases. First, you must become aware of tension and relaxation and the way the muscles feel in each of these states. Next, you need to learn how to breathe properly and comfortably through your diaphragm. Finally, you need a formula or process to guide you into a state of complete relaxation.

Tension and Relaxation.   Lie on a bed or sit in a comfortable chair in a quiet room where you won't be interrupted for 15 minutes or so. Begin by clenching your fists. Focus first on the feelings and sensations you have in your wrists and forearms. Then consider your entire body. Does your breathing change? Do your stomach muscles tighten? Pay attention to all the sensations you feel. This is tension—the tight, hard, strong feelings.

Now relax your hand, shake it gently, and become aware of the changes you feel. Feel the muscles loosen up and get lighter as the tension leaves. Do the clenching and relaxing process again, becoming more aware of the two states. Do the same exercise with your legs. Notice the changes and become aware of how your muscles feel when they are relaxed.

Diaphragmatic Breathing.   Again, do this exercise lying down in a quiet room where you are comfortable and will not be interrupted for 15 or 20 minutes. While lying on your back, place your hand high on your abdomen, just below the rib cage. Take a deep breath. Watch your hand. Which way did it move? Up, down, not at all? If you are a diaphragmatic breather, your hand will move up. If you are a thoracic breather, your hand will move only slightly, if at all.

Diaphragmatic breathing works like this. Exhale, emptying your lungs completely. Take a deep breath. As you inhale, place your hand on your abdomen and monitor the breathing pattern as follows. The lower abdomen expands, creating a vacuum in the chest cavity and causing air to be drawn into the lower lungs. As the middle section of the lungs fills, your upper abdomen expands. While you continue inhaling, filling your lungs with air, your chest expands to fill the upper regions of your lungs.

Exhale and empty your lungs completely. Take a deep breath. Did you inhale through your nose or mouth? Exhale. Did you use your nose or mouth? Now practice breathing in through your nose, even if it is not your normal method, and exhaling through your mouth. Put them together with the inhaling sequence for diaphragmatic breathing, and you are ready for the next step.

Relaxation Formula.   The following is a short reference list for perfecting a smooth and rhythmic relaxation routine. Adapt it to fit your needs or insert key words that help you relax and clear your mind.

Relaxation Routine

Take three deep diaphragmatic breaths.

Feel the tension in your face and let it evaporate until your face is smooth and relaxed.

Let your arms and legs get limp, heavy, and warm as they begin to relax.

Your arms and legs are becoming heavier and warmer as the muscles get looser and looser.

Your arms and legs are completely heavy and warm.

Your heartbeat is calm and steady.

You feel supremely calm and relaxed.

Your stomach is soft and warm.

You feel supremely calm and relaxed.

Your forehead is cool and comfortable.

You feel supremely calm and relaxed.

These steps may seem simple. Like all skills, however, they take practice and time to master. As you gain mastery, you will find that you can induce a hypnotic state by simply sitting down and taking the three diaphragmatic breaths while thinking about the formula for relaxation.

6. Attention Control

Attention control is your ability to manage distractions while focusing attention on the appropriate variables while skiing. Distractions are anything that draws your attention away from the task at hand—skiing. You want to be 100 percent attentive to what you are trying to do on the water, ignoring factors that do not contribute to the successful completion of your ski ride. If you have good attention control you remain focused on the feelings, movements, and visual cues that allow you to compete successfully. If your attention control is weak, you may find that factors pop up during or before your event that easily distract you.

Distractions during competition may be either internal or external. Internal distractions include any thoughts or feelings that draw you away from your focus. Skiers who are internally distracted may find themselves paying attention to internal dialogue or feelings. These skiers pay attention to their self-talk, thoughts of technical position, feelings of anxiety or fatigue, or other internal cues.

External distractions include any outside stimuli that draw your attention away from the task at hand. Changes in water conditions, other skiers, fans, boat speed or path, and even the type of rope being used are examples of external distractions. By practicing the skill of attention control, mentally tough skiers do not allow themselves to lose their focus for any extended period because of uncontrollable factors. Skiers with poor attention control will become fixated on these distractions and will shift their focus away from the more critical factors such as rhythm, location on the gates, and peak of the wake.

Readiness.   You can maximize your performance by minimizing your attention to potential distractions and improving your concentration and decision-making skills on the water. One key to effective attention control can be summed up in the word "readiness." How often are you 100 percent ready to ski before your event? Readiness is the critical variable that guides your attention throughout an event. If you are totally ready then your attention will be drawn to the event, and you will become mentally engaged in it. But if you simply go through the motions of warming up, and prepare haphazardly for your event, internal thoughts and external factors will creep into your mind. A focused mind has little room for visitors! Peak performers consistently report that their best performances come when they focus entirely on the here and now, giving no attention to the past or future. Keep your mind focused on what you are doing in the moment. You will find that the skills that you work so hard to develop in practice will be there on tournament day.

Simulation Training.   To help develop better attention control, try using the strategy of simulation training. The goal of simulation training is to develop the mental and physical ability to deal with external factors of distraction. Often, the external factors are the cause of the internal factors, so this type of training is helpful for improving your attention control. The key is to identify situations that may cause you difficulty during competition and simulate those conditions in practice. When practicing under simulated conditions take careful mental notes of the methods that are effective in coping with distractions. Practice them often. Over time you will become aware of the thoughts, feelings, and mental pictures you can use effectively to maintain attention control. Make mental and written notes of these strategies and take control of your performances. Here are some things to try:

1. Conduct minitournaments with your training partners. To turn on the heat, throw in $20 each or set up some consequence for not meeting your goal, such as washing the boat. Use handicaps to keep things fair.
2. Run tournament sets in practice. Allow no do-overs. You have to swim in after a fall, and you must pay some consequence if you do not meet your goal.
3. If you are frustrated, tired, or doubt yourself during a practice session, have a tournament set right then and learn how to refocus your mind and thoughts to a positive direction.
4. Have a person in the boat or on shore try to distract you by yelling or waving at you during your set.
5. Have others make distracting comments about the boat path, boat speed, water conditions, or wind, or instruct the driver to drive badly so that you learn how to deal with it.
6. Have special people in your life watch you during simulated tournament sets.
7. Vary practice times and conditions, boat drivers, time between sets, or permit yourself no warm-up.

Re-create any situation in which you have had problems and learn how to deal with it. Make it a game and practice it often; it can be fun and rewarding.

7. Intensity Management

Intensity management refers to your ability to manage your physiological and mental intensity throughout the day of competition. To maximize your physical and technical potential, you must be able to manage performance anxiety and competitive pressure during competition. Your ability to remain relaxed, calm, and alert while competing in an event will affect your performance. Skiers who are excellent intensity managers are in tune with their bodies; they know when they are getting too pumped up or nervous. Additionally, these skiers are also alert enough to catch themselves when they are getting too relaxed, bored, or tired.

Top skiers are aware of the intensity level at which their bodies best function. Think back to a day when you felt you were skiing your best. On a scale of 1 (sleeping) to 10 (overanxious), how intense were you during your event that day? Can you re-create that intensity and manage it until it is time for your event?

There are three keys to intensity management.

1. Being aware of your ideal intensity level or peak performance zone
2. Being able to identify when you have moved out of your zone, toward either boredom or anxiety
3. Being able to increase or decrease your intensity to a point that is in your zone

You may find you have a different intensity zone for each event. Skiers generally report that they feel more intense during jump than during slalom. Once you have identified your ideal intensity level, you can develop strategies that will help you gain and regulate your intensity during competition. The precompetition warm-up is one of the most effective strategies I have found to develop intensity management. It combines many of the peak-performance factors we have just discussed into a format that you can use to prepare for a peak performance.

PRECOMPETITION WARM-UP

The ultimate measure of athletic greatness is consistency. From Carl Roberge, Sherri Slone, Rhoni Barton, Wade Cox, Kristi Overton, and the LaPoints to Jack Nicklaus, Michael Jordan, and Steffi Graf, one element is always the same—a remarkable level of performance consistency under all circumstances. These athletes have the special ability to control the process of performing toward the upper range of their capabilities. The distinguishing trademark of skiers and athletes such as these is not so much their exceptional talent, but their exceptional ability to play consistently at the peak of their talent. The question is not how these exceptional performers achieve this control but how you can gain control of the peak-performance process. The precompetition warm-up ritual is a strategy you can implement into your training to gain peak-performance consistency.

Every good performer has rituals. Some are more obvious and elaborate than others. You have seen them at the free-throw line, on the pitcher's mound, in the batter's box, on a serve in tennis, and in a golf swing. These sometimes bizarre mannerisms are unrelated to the mechanics of the activity, but can become powerful triggers for creating the mental state of peak performance. Rituals help in deepening concentration, turning on the automatic pilot, raising intensity, staying loose, and developing a mindset with high positive energy that gives you the best probability of a good performance.

By using these rituals, skiers achieve their ideal performance state (IPS). You can learn to reach your IPS by monitoring yourself and tracking your scores. Use the rating sheet on page 215 to determine how you feel before, during, and after a ski session. By collecting this information you will begin to see patterns in your performances and be able to relate them to how you felt or warmed up before the event. Once you know what your IPS is then you simply learn to re-create or reenact those thoughts and feelings. The following is a recommended precompetition warm-up routine that several national and world champion skiers have used to attain their IPS. Try it out in practice, make adjustments, and then use it in competition. No matter what you do, find a ritual that gets you to your IPS, and you will become a more consistent peak performer.

Phase I: Intensity Management

Warm-up. Begin by doing 5 to 10 minutes of light aerobic activity (walk, jog, jumping jacks) to raise your body temperature and remove nervous energy. Research has shown that peak performances occur when muscle temperature is slightly elevated while heart rate remains normal, so the next step of the warm-up phase is to bring your heart rate down by doing some stretching (see chapter 3 for suggested stretches). Be careful not to overstretch because doing so has been shown to cause the muscles to react more slowly.

Phase II: Mental Rehearsal and Visualization

The awesome power of visualization and mental rehearsal is well documented. Mental imaging is a difficult skill that must be practiced. These tips will make the process easier. Sit in a quiet, comfortable place and relax for several moments. Take three deep breaths, allowing your lungs to fill until your stomach extends outward. When your body is relaxed, create a mental movie of the perfect slalom set, jump, or trick run. Try to use as many senses as possible. Feel the water, hear the boat and the fans, smell the air. Mentally rehearse the positive feelings you wish to have and make detailed and complete images, filling in more details as you go. If unrelated thoughts, feelings, or ideas intrude, relax and put them aside by creating a new image for the mental rehearsal. You should practice this process two or three times a week.

Phase III: Attention Control

Quiet your mind as you visualize your ski ride. Your mind will become focused, turning your attention toward your ski performance and away

IPS RATING SHEET

Name ———————————— Date ————— Time —————

1. Muscles relaxed	1	2	3	4	5	Muscles tight
2. Calm and quiet	1	2	3	4	5	Fast and frantic
3. Low anxiety	1	2	3	4	5	High anxiety
4. High energy	1	2	3	4	5	Low energy
5. Positive	1	2	3	4	5	Negative
6. Highly enjoyable	1	2	3	4	5	Unenjoyable
7. Effortless	1	2	3	4	5	Great effort
8. Automatic	1	2	3	4	5	Deliberate
9. Confident	1	2	3	4	5	Not confident
10. Alert	1	2	3	4	5	Dull
11. In control	1	2	3	4	5	Out of control
12. Focused	1	2	3	4	5	Unfocused
13. Played well	1	2	3	4	5	Played poorly
14. Positive energy	1	2	3	4	5	Negative energy

Comments:

_____

_____

_____

_____

_____

_____

_____

_____

_____

from the events of the day. As this focus improves, stop creating the mental imagery. Trust that you have prepared your mind and that the images you have created are complete. As thoughts, ideas, or feelings enter your mind, let them go. Your first priority right now is to quiet your mind by letting go of all thoughts, ideas, and feelings that come to your attention by either committing them to memory or letting them fade into the distance.

Phase IV: Energy Focus

Rid yourself of negative thoughts. If negative thoughts or feelings arise, relax and deal with them. You need not panic or worry—negative thoughts pop up in everyone's mind. The trick is how you deal with them. An effective way of eliminating negative thoughts is visualizing the thought being eaten up by a Pac Man. Another way is to visualize writing the thought on a chalkboard and erasing it, or writing it on a piece of paper and burning it. The key is first to acknowledge the thought in a calm state of mind and then remove it in a manner that is comfortable.

Phase V: Thought Control

Focus on the present. As your mind becomes more clear, allow your attention to turn toward the reality of the present moment. Focus on your senses. Focus on the loudness of the boat or the soft rhythm of the waves hitting the shore. Notice the colors of the sky, the tint of the water. Feel the texture of the handle in your hand and the coolness of the water. The key to focusing on the present is learning to be attentive to your senses, to the quality of what you are sensing rather than your interpretation of the meaning. As you come off the dock go trustingly. Trust that you have prepared your mind and body to function at their best. Trust that you can turn off your analytical left brain and give control to your visual right brain. By doing this you will turn on your built-in "computer" that will guide you to a perfect performance. All you have to do is get out of the way and allow your mind and body to come together as one and function at optimal levels.

Like every valuable skill, you must practice your precompetition warm-up routine and make it part of your competition-day plan. You must be sure to take enough time to prepare before your event so you do not rush or skip part of your warm-up. Know how long you need to arrive before your event and how long before you ski so you have time to go through your warm-up routine properly. Study the rituals of top skiers and learn from them; they serve as excellent models. By determining the best plan for you, you can control the controllable and deal with the uncontrollable in a relaxed, positive manner that leads to consistent peak performances.

Figure 9.2   The key to focusing on the present is learning to be attentive to your senses.

FINE-TUNING YOUR SKIING SKILLS

Every champion has gotten some help along the path to success. None of us can accomplish our goals without the support of family, friends, coaches, and trainers. You can't do it alone. Similarly, there is no such thing as an overnight success. Every champion spent hours in the gym and on the water developing the strength, coordination, and concentration to become a winner. Rome wasn't built in a day and neither is a champion. All athletes must work constantly on their talent foundation to get to the top and must work even harder to stay there. The process is extremely dynamic. You must constantly tweak your training program to improve your weaknesses. Three final training strategies or ideas will help you accomplish your goals in skiing.

BUILDING YOUR SUPPORT TEAM

Any foundation must have support, including your talent foundation. Your support team members are the pilings on which you lay your foundation. This team works behind the scene, providing encouragement and motivation that you can't do without. Your support team can be just your spouse or parents, or it can be an entourage of physicians, therapists, trainers, physiologists, biomechanists, sport psychologists, sport nutritionists, and coaches like that used by tennis superstar Martina Navratilova. The key element of a support team is communication, and the coach is the conductor of the orchestra. You should choose a coach with the same care you would use to select a surgeon. You wouldn't want someone to operate on you just because he or she was polite or had a fancy office. Yet this is how many people select a coach. Find a coach who can assess your qualities and find the best path for your success. As the team leader, the coach should have a fundamental knowledge of sports medicine and sports science so he or she can design a training program that helps you avoid injury and maximizes on- and off-water time.

When I decided to quit my job and ski professionally, the first thing I did was find a coach who fit this description. Jay Bennett was, and still is, an integral source of wisdom and motivation for me. With a top-quality coach in place, I began setting up the other pieces of my support team. The idea is simple; if you want to compete with the best skiers in the world you need to have the best support team. Some members of my support team are books I've read, others are people I worked with, but all were coordinated through my coach. Much of this book is derived from the ideas, theories, and inspiration of my support-team members. Your support team should consist of people you are comfortable with, people who want you to succeed, and most important, people you can communicate with.

OPTIMIZING YOUR PERFORMANCES

If you want to ski at the top level, learning to periodize your training is extremely valuable. Periodization is a long-term training plan designed to optimize peak performances—it will help you control when, where, and how often you peak. Amateur and pro athletes from a variety of sports have used periodization with outstanding results. In this section, we'll give you an idea of how to periodize a water skiing training schedule.

You must first realize that neither you nor any other athlete is able to maintain a peak level of performance for much more than a three-week period. And you can't train all out year-round. Periodization means building a training program around when you want to peak. You must learn to balance and intertwine the variables of training volume, intensity, and frequency to fit the schedule of when you want to ski your best.

Periodization training helps to avoid overtraining and staleness by varying the program throughout the season. The periodization scheme breaks the season into four macrocycles (preparation, preseason, competition, and active rest). These macrocycles are subdivided into microcycles lasting four to six weeks; microcycles help you achieve as many peaks as you need. Each macro and microcycle should have specific goals and training strategies that will lead to success.

Preparation Phase

For water skiing, this phase lasts from about January 1 until February 15. It starts two to three months before the season begins. The goal during this phase is to improve physical fitness, emphasizing muscular strength, cardiorespiratory strength, and endurance. All forms of training in this phase focus on high-volume, low-intensity work. For strength training use light weight and high repetitions across a wide variety of exercises. Your skiing training should focus on the fundamentals, with the goal of getting in as many reps or passes as you can. The preparation phase is also a great time for cross training in other sports and for improving your speed and agility. Table 10.1 gives the steps to success in this phase.

Table 10.1   Preparation Phase

Fitness testing
Aerobic conditioning
Strength and flexibility
Anaerobic conditioning
Speed and agility

Precompetitive Phase

This phase occurs from about mid-February until mid-April. The goal of this phase is to intensify training routines so they approximate the demands of your event. The objective is to achieve the metabolism, movement, and muscle specificity you use on the water when skiing. The training focuses on achieving maximum power with anaerobic endurance and speed. During this transition phase, the training loads move toward higher intensities and lower volumes. Train with high intensity and explosive exercises for both weight and aerobic drills. Your skiing should balance challenging passes or drills with endurance skiing to continue to build strength. This phase should last four to six weeks. This is the time to use video to make technical changes and to use on-water drills to improve your weaknesses. Table 10.2 gives you the steps to success for this stage of your training.

Table 10.2   Precompetitive Phase

> Skiing skills assessment and testing
> Technical changes and improvements
> Video analysis
> On-water drills

Competitive Peaking Phase

This phase lasts from roughly mid-April through mid-September. During this phase, athletes try to bring out their optimal performance during competition and develop the competition skills needed for success. You must plan peaking carefully to strike a balance between overtraining, which leads to burnout and injuries, and undertraining, which means you won't be at your best. A true peak can last only three weeks, as we stated earlier, but you can prolong it by scheduling rest periods between competitions. Strength training during this phase consists of one hard workout per week that will overload the muscles. Cut back cardio work to maintenance volumes. On-water training concentrates on technique and developing mental toughness through the use of strategy development and tournament simulation. The steps to building the skills needed to peak are given in table 10.3.

Table 10.3   Competitive Peaking Phase

> Mental toughness evaluation
> Skiing strategy assessment
> Tournament strategy/tactic development
> Mental skills simulation training
> Tournament peak skiing

Active Rest Phase

This phase occurs just as the season has ended. It is a time for total rest of one to four weeks followed by a light maintenance conditioning program. During the total rest period you should do only light stretching and aerobic work. The idea is to rest mentally and physically so you're ready when you gear up for the upcoming season.

Figure 10.1 is a conceptual model of a season-long periodization schedule. The tournament simulation line represents the intensity of your practice, or how closely you should duplicate what you do in competition. The conditioning/technique line represents your volume of practice, or the amount of time you should spend training and conditioning yourself physically. As you move closer to competition, your focus should shift from conditioning and technique practice to tournament simulation and mental toughness training. If your competitive phase needs to last longer than three weeks, develop minicycles within each month or week. An example would be to pick certain tournaments each year that you "train for" (desire to peak at) and others that you "train through" (ski without concern for performance but work on certain aspects of your skiing). To extend a peak period for longer than three weeks, you need to focus intensely on the mental aspects of training and have the discipline to reduce your conditioning and technique training dramatically. You should never try to peak for longer than six weeks without taking some time to regroup and cycle yourself back up through a minicycle. To do this, begin by taking one to three days of complete rest followed by three to five days of conditioning and technique work. Once you feel strong and rested mentally and physically, begin another peaking phase, focusing on mental toughness and tournament simulation.

USING A TRAINING LOG

Tracking your progress is a vital part of your training. Your training log serves as a subconscious motivator when you see that you are or aren't meeting your training goals. It can be helpful in reproducing results

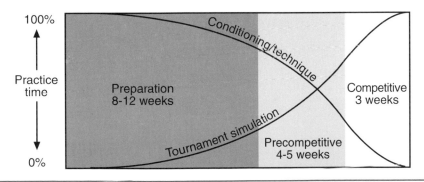

Figure 10.1   Season-long periodization schedule.

and setting your next goal after you accomplish your first one. The training log is also a great way to get your feelings out. Use it to vent all the negative stuff that may have come up during your training or work day. By freeing your mind of negative thoughts you're able to think positively and objectively. Think of your training log as a progress report. You'll be able to see changes in the mental, physical, and technical aspects of your skiing. After grading yourself, jot down any notes about the day, your mood, the workout or tournament. Express both the positive and negative feelings and how you dealt with them. Most important, take detailed notes of successes, whether they are on the water, in the gym, or in your head. A sample form you can use in preparing your training log appears on page 225.

Fine-tuning your training program is an ongoing and ever-changing process that will contribute to your success. If you miss a day of training due to injury or other commitment, don't fret, don't try to make it up; simply pick things up on the next scheduled day and get after it. Missing one day of training need not snowball into slacking off on mental training or another element of training that isn't affected by the injury or time constraint. Make the needed changes in your plan and go on, taking one step at a time and enjoying each success on the way to achieving your goal of skiing better.

Sports psychologist James Lohr, EdD says, "It all begins with a dream for the future, and it all happens with what you do today." Whether you are a self-proclaimed river rat as I was when growing up, or a Pro Tour competitor as I am now, you can attain your dreams in water skiing by using the step-by-step, skills-based approach laid out for you here. Use this program each time you want to make that step to the next level of performance. Every dream that becomes a reality begins with the thought that you can achieve it. From that point on, it's up to you.

DAILY TRAINING LOG

	MON	TUE	WED	THU	FRI	SAT	SUN
1. Aerobic exercise (time)							
2. Interval anaerobic exercise (time)							
3. Sit-ups (number)							
4. Strength training (time)							
5. Stretching (y/n)							
6. Diet (A - F grade)							
7. Number of meals							
8. Quantity of sleep (hours)							
9. Quality of sleep (1-10)							
10. Time to bed/time up							
11. Nap (yes/no)							
12. Visualization practice (time)							
13. Overall volume of stress (1-10)							
14. Quantity of recovery (time)							
15. Quality of recovery (1-10)							
16. Tough thinking (A - F)							
17. Tough acting (A - F)							
18. Patient (A - F)							
19. Independent (A - F)							
20. Stress/recovery balance (1-10)							
21. Felt energy, motivation, fun (1-10)							
22. Disciplined (A - F)							
23. Relaxation tape (time)							
24. How well performed today (1-10)							
25. Got tougher today (y/n)							

ABOUT THE AUTHORS

Ben Favret, a nationally known water ski professional and instructor, began skiing at the age of four. By the time he was 13, he was skiing in local tournaments; soon he moved up to the regional and national level, winning the 1994 Open National Slalom Championship.

After earning his bachelor's degree in marketing from the University of Alabama in 1987, Favret worked in sales and marketing. Leaving his job to pursue his professional skiing career, he worked the Pro Tour circuit and became an American Water Ski Association (AWSA) Level I instructor and the head coach at Bennett's Water Ski School in

Zachary, Louisiana. He has coached the U.S. Junior team as well as teams from Germany, New Zealand, and Japan. Favret writes extensively for *Water Ski, The Water Skier, Water Ski Illustrated,* and *Ski Nautique.* On the AWSA Board of Directors and member of the Professional Association of Slalom Skiers, Favret continues to live in Zachary, where he enjoys playing basketball, golf, and tennis.

David Benzel has been involved with water skiing for more than 25 years as an athlete, coach, author, business owner, and parent of young champions.

A six-time national champion and five-time record holder, Benzel is the former coach of the World Champion U.S. Water Ski Team. As a motivational speaker, Benzel applies coaching concepts to the workplace, speaking to business organizations on topics such as personal peak performance, leadership, and team building. Author of the book *Psyching For Slalom,* he also writes a monthly column entitled "Head Coach" for *Water Ski Magazine.*

Benzel founded the Benzel Skiing Center, which opened in 1985. He is chairman of the board for the American Water Ski Education Foundation and is on the AWSA's Board of Directors. He has organized several water skiing clinics and symposiums, including the Junior Develop national and regional clinics, the National Coaching Symposiums, and the water skiing "Super Seminar" at the U.S. Olympic Training Center. Benzel also provides color commentary for water skiing events on ESPN.

He and his wife, Cynthia, live in Groveland, Florida, with their two children—Tarah, already a 5-time champion at age 12, and Tyler, who started competing at the age of 6. When he's not water skiing, Benzel enjoys in-line skating, playing baseball with his children, biking, and reading.